OFF THE CUFFS:
POETRY BY AND ABOUT THE POLICE

EDITED BY JACKIE SHEELER
FOREWORD BY BOB HOLMAN

2003
SOFT SKULL PRESS
BROOKLYN, NY

Off the Cuffs: Poetry by and about the Police
isbn: 1-887128-81-6
©2003 Jackie Sheeler.

First Edition

Cover Design and Illustration: NOUNCREATIVE.COM
Interior Design: DAVID JANIK
Editorial: DANIEL NESTER

Distributed by Publishers Group West
1 800 788 3123 | WWW.PGW.COM

Printed in Canada

Soft Skull Press
71 Bond Street
Brooklyn, NY 11217
WWW.SOFTSKULL.COM

CONTENTS

II: VICTIMS & PERPETRATORS

III: INSIDERS

IV: DREAMERS   241

Dedicated to George Jaccarino,
NYPD patrolman (retired)

BOB HOLMAN

dean of scene

FOREWORD

Off the Cuffs is an imagining.

Imagine a world where we don't play cops'n'robbers nor von Suppe's "Poet And Peasant Overture,"[1] but a world where cops *are* poets, digging deeply into language emotion art constructs, and poets *are* police, dealing daily with crime victim punishment muck.

Can't imagine? That's OK. Neither could Plato.

Back in the day, in his Ideal State, Plato the Anti-Poet[2] saw the police (and the army) as the "middle" section of society: the "Auxiliaries" between the "Producers" (masses) and the "Guardians" (righteous leaders). The Auxiliaries had "Courage" and the Guardians "Wisdom"; the Producers were characterized by "Obedience." A state has "temperance" when the Auxiliaries obey the Guardians in all things and the Producers obey the Auxiliaries and Guardians in all things—which is why Plato kicked the provocative, language-slinging Poets out of the Republic.

And it's taken til this anthology to re-imagine Plato's paradigm. Jackie Sheeler dares to unite the exiled uncontrollable poets and their opposite, society's watchdogs, the police. This is not a themed literature anthology: it's a new way of looking at society. Through the lens of *Off the Cuffs* you'll glimpse a place where everyone's a poet, and a cop, too. A mind-stretch, not a metaphor. It's mutual respect. And it's an equation for an Ideal State that's not, as Plato's was, built on the backs of slaves.[3]

Off the Cuffs—great title!— marks the end of poetry's First Big Step into the Center of U.S. discourse. The 1990's marked the beginning of a turn-around for poetry, heretofore an endangered species.[4] A renewed interest in the sound of poetry, in the poetry reading, has emerged with the popularity of hip-hop and slam, performance and spoken word. The acceptance of media-as-book has brought poetry into lives and living rooms through poetry videos and CD's. And the globalization-via-Web dynamic has allowed local scenes to discover like-minded poets, outside of official lineages, and build connections beyond the academically sanctioned. The Web has also made it possible to publish for free, with instanter[5] distribution. The world is discovering, directly, the way poets speak from within a culture in a way that doesn't "represent," but somehow *is* the living text of that culture. Poetry is becoming relevant. Take that, Mr. Plato!

Off the Cuffs is also a sign.

A sign that U.S. poetry is shrugging off the shackles of aestheticism and picking up the tools of utility. A sign that the working person, the Average Jose and Josie, isn't the presumed uncultured nonsophisticate, isn't necessarily anti-culture/pro-TV, and doesn't buy into poetry as a pastime of the elite. Poetry, in fact, is leading the way in allowing folks to participate, firsthand, in U.S. culture.

And so instead of recent publication credits of the authors and so forth, you get each poet labeled by their day job. A dance critic, a social worker, a bike messenger, an insurance investigator, a calligrapher, an editor. Detectives, patrolmen/women, sheriffs, DA's, cops and their brothers, fathers, wives, husbands, grandfathers, children. You get the ex-wife of an ex-cop. A cop in drag, or rather, a man in cop drag.

This is the only anthology I've seen where poets choose to be known as "Teacher," "Lawyer," "Anonymous," "Cultural Activist," or "Character Witness." There are others whose names I don't recognize, and whose "Anonymous" professions can be explained if the stories of illegal enterprise are true. Being labeled a Poet seems equivalent to Blackmailer or Strong Arm Robber.

To out a few poets, then. Jack Agüeros. Janine Pommy Vega, who as a teacher in prisons notes "I'm locked in, too" in "C.O." Martín Espada. Sharon Olds. Colette Inez (from "Slumnight": "the moon pulls up/in a squad car"). Hettie Jones, who also teaches in prison, knows she has "made it" when she's on "The Semipermanent Gate List." Diane di Prima. D.H. Melhem. Douglas Rothschild, who even incorporates the New York School tradition of shouting out to another poet, in this case Anselm Berrigan. Tony Medina's amazing reconstruction of the O.J. Bronco trail ride, with cameos by Jimmy Hoffa, Rodney King, and Jesus. Muriel Rukeyser deftly, painfully, pulls walls down, builds them up—which begs the question: Do poets create their own prisons? W.S. Merwin's fox—a symbol of? And Anne Waldman, whose heroic panegyric kicks off *Off the Cuffs* like a siren that never stops, never goes away.

Stephen Dobyns' "The Great Doubters of History" is a breathtaking inversion of Bobby McGee's "Nothin' left to lose": "In fact, it seems the point of society is to/make people think they have something to lose," concluding with a trope that fills your lungs with amazement. Sometimes the poets get it right. When Maggie Dubris writes from the front seat of her paramedic emergency vehicle and sees the killer of a patient in "Willieworld," the poetry matches the shock.

Perhaps my favorite piece is Ed Sanders' extraordinary investigative poetry epic, *1968*, where he tells the tale of "Pigasus," the Yippie presidential nominee that year and a real pig. Sanders discusses the dehumanizing of cops in the 60's battle cry, "Off the pigs!" and gives the historic antecedent: Austrian Futurists, who called gendarmes "walking pissoirs."

The poets' takes on the subject are so varied, in fact, that when a non-poet imagines a poetic response, you realize the role that poetry has assumed in the culture is *not* the way poetry works in the culture. Detective William Hladky questions a suspect in "Weeping Walls" and writes that "a proper poet would hold you tight, but I'm not a proper poet." Later in the poem he says "I will hug you/(but not too tightly)/to get you to confess/to convict your ass." There are police in South Africa, cops who move to the rescue to remove a deer from a tree. A cop gives a driving test. "Kneiveled" is a verb in Patricia Callan's "Road Test." A squad car speaks to us, thanks to Police Officer J.J. Camp.

It may take awhile for the book to work on you. Often the subjects are so grim— you're sucked into the horrendous dailiness of cops and can't find the poetry. That's our problem. All of a sudden, *Off the Cuffs* becomes a contemporary *Canterbury Tales* from Hell! Story after story offers angles on the culture so complex that it's downright trigonometry—most often these poems are concerned with crime and its consequences, no punch pulled. Hell has been tamed, though—or at least civilized enough so you can read it—by the Editor's keen eye, her surprising attention to form. Sheeler is way open to content/style variety and focuses our attention on how these poems speak to each other, break down barriers. She's the daughter of a cop, he was a good father. Get it?

She will, for instance, arrange by actual poetic form to make some points. Sestinas and sonnets and villanelles and balletic spacing with no caps—and not from the "poet" poets, either! And there are forms of crimes: from generic philosophic to racial "My body is the color of protection." From rape and murder to parking to a busted taillight. And then there's the content/form mix: a pantoum in which we all seem to be the suspect, a sonnet about a woman hiding a knife under her breast, a found poem of a call-in show, a slam poem about getting stopped for speeding, a new media poem about getting yourself busted, and a haiku about a cop in a mirror.

There are even the rich moments when life itself teaches us about poetic technique. Denise Duhamel teaches her students the definition of "irony" and "metaphor," and a student, just returning to class after two days in jail, another false arrest of a young Black male, stands up and takes a bow—"the best definition we could come up with."

This is the book where the rape victim speaks for herself in Linda Lanza's "Mining for Eureka." Where Sarah Cortez, a cop who dates cops, lets us in on the special "Lingo," where *fuck you* "means hello."

One of the joys of this book is comparing form and heart, content and scream, as the purposes of poetry collide. Some examples.

Rhyme, as handled by poet Thom Gunn, breaking fast as a gunshot:

Such cops would view themselves as al-
    legorical
Unaltered by what they had done
    So long as one,
At a dusk somewhere, in the cells,
    Or somewhere else
(In heaven?), could tell a sting
    From the real thing

...to rhyme, as handled by military police officer Rodger L. Hilliard, sing-songy hip-hop influenced:

I be the Po-Po, the Five-O
but you can call me...Bro'
yo' ass in a fix...
I be the one you oughta know

Other comparisons set up by Ms. Sheeler's selection of poems that converse with each other, as if the reader is overhearing. To get a feel, check out one sequence in which the seesaw of justice teeters from authors Kaufman to McManus (pages 144–154) in which she pit cops with criminals, victims with pigs. Other times, you'll enter the enemy's terrain, and eventually realize how we're all in the human game. She'll see-saw you til you get vertigo—til your brain starts to make the kind of leaps poetry demands.

From "South Central Cheap Thrills" by Cultural Activist Wanda Coleman:

you have not lived
until two uniforms knock on your door
at sunrise with a warrant for your arrest
because you did not pay
that poot-butt parking ticket
because what little money you earn
goes first to the landlord,
second to feed your kids the sugar, salt and starch
they need to keep breathing

is followed by Detective William Hladky:

Let me write this down.
Would you mind if we go over your story again with a tape recorder?
You would protect yourself putting it on tape.
I won't be able to change anything when I write my report.
Don't you feel better?

Cops do get a chance to tell their side of the story, a job which, in real life, is usually handled by the Department. The Thin Blue Line that divides populace from police fades as cops become individuals, become poets. In a poem by Police Officer Corbet Dean, he attempts to get it all in there. He starts off and calls himself an asshole. He asks his son if he wants to be an asshole, that if he grows up to be a cop he'll be one, because "all cops are assholes." Then he tells two sparse, personal stories of his police work. They both involve child abuse and murder, and are so horrifying that the reader can choose between vomiting and saying this poem is overwritten, sentimental, *blah blah blah*, while vomiting. Then you see the poem is titled "Letter My Dad Never Gave Me." It's from *his own* father, not to his son. Or maybe it's a poem that he's writing for his son. Or both. This is the insider poem on being a police officer, of being the asshole of society, where the shit is. And it's not pretty. Somehow this poem, especially because he's trying to get it all in, creates a zone of understanding that's downright physical.

And a few pages later, Morty Sklar, a publisher, composes a poem around the repeated phrase, "It's a cultural thing." In it, he bashes liberals, everyday inconsiderates, people who attack police for no reason, and a mayor who blames the victim. This extraordinary litany shows a range of other "assholes," that weaves together, in a most politically incorrect way, our whole culture, and shows how unaware we all can be of the need for cops. He calls the poem "Culture," and makes you wish there was more of it.

OK, let's just take a "Cop Poem," that is, a poem by a cop. What is it that Patrolman Phillip Mahoney is writing about? A poetry reading. That he gave. In a prison. From "On Giving a Poetry Reading at Arthur Kill Correctional Facility":

the walls between us
are not made of stone
but of circumstance.

This is the Landscape where Cops are Poets and Poets are Cops: It's a landscape most of us will never know, where expectations vanish in a gunshot or a strange alliance. New ways of seeing when you take off the cuffs: "Cops come slow as love" (Daphne Gottlieb, "Deer Prudence"). Busted street merchants selling self-picked flowers and snow cones. Dailiness in a morgue. The impossibility of forgetting a forgotten woman who died alone, as in "Above a Darkened Bed," Scott Odom, Deputy Sheriff. "LC," a love crime, not a hate crime, for Maggie Balistreri. Cops testifying, bringing you the horrors that define their jobs: the rape of a newborn, standing guard over the body of a young suicide victim who jumped. "Compassion"—overheard on the subway—the precinct house attack on Abner Louima a crime. The shooting of Amadou Diallo, an error. A five-page poem about an illegal car search, by a victim of racial profiling in "Blackman Brotherman & the Highway Patrolman." Danna Botwick drops Daddy off at jail and searches for the right words to answer her daughter's "I want Daddy/NOW!/ I wish daddy didn't do that bad/thing in the first place!" A professor finds himself in jail and is asked to read a poem. Charles Rammelkamp takes us to the street in "On the Beat," where a young cop whose squad car won't start watches the "meanest-looking dude on the corner" pop his trunk and pull out—jumper cables.

And so by the time Sheeler introduces the "Insiders" section, we start to get it: this is not a play on words about the imprisoned, but two species who inhabit a prison: the guarded and the guards, "two species inhabit the gray stone/black steel skeleton of prison: the guarded and the guards. Everybody's doing time."

There is currently a crisis in the prison system. We're only now beginning to slow the growth industry of building prisons. It's been a significant indicator of the economic boom—we're building prisons at a rate faster than schools.⁶ This book is a sign that there are indicators other than the economic ones, that you cannot solve problems by locking people up behind walls, out of sight, and forgetting.

And there's a crisis in poetry world, too. It's the perpetual scratching for survival of an art form that's always been with us, which in the U.S. has never found a comfortable spot to speak from, and has been defined as pretty much elitist.

This is the book that takes the crises in law enforcement, in our prison system, in grass-roots arts movements, and in the state of U.S. poetry in general, and tries to make sense of them all—using poetry. *Off the Cuffs* is a liberating, visionary approach to what makes our society sick, and also what makes it tick. It's a blueprint for a Utopia that's reachable. Read the book, think, and then get busy.

---

¹ Von Suppe was a famous "light" classical composer of the 19th century. This reference is not here for the sake of aparallelism: this extraordinary overture was used in many Looney Tunes' "Silly Symphonies." Give an ear—you'll be amazed. It can also, heh heh, be heard on my Mouth Almighty CD, *In With the Out Crowd*, in the poem "Forgotten Melody."

² If you want more Plato, I'd recommend the writings of Richard Hooker.

³ Unless you want to analyze the "underclass" as "slaves." The underclass— criminals created by the Guardians, resulting in the growth industry of prisons. There are more young Black males in prison than in college.

⁴ Now, I know plenty of poets will leap into battle over this assertion. I doubt that many cops would, however. Which is what I'm talking about. "Endangered" does not that mean poetry is about to disappear altogether; it simply means that poetry has disappeared from most people's lives. IMHO, there are great poets alive today, and terrific poems are being written. But I'm a poet, it's my job, and I love the stuff. For most citizens, however, poetry exists somewhere else. I'm saying this is changing.

⁵ See "Projective Verse" by Charles Olson (1950).

⁶ Programs like PEN's Prison Initiative gets the word into and out of jail through workshops. See poems by Hettie Jones, Janine Pommy Vega, and Colette Inez.

OFF THE CUFFS:

POETRY BY AND ABOUT THE POLICE

EYEWITNESSES

The people are watching the cops. The perps are watching the cops. The cops are watching the cops. The brothers and spouses and grandchildren of cops are watching the cops, comparing their uniformed and uninformed selves.

I have watched the cops for most of my life—my father first put on his NYPD uniform the same year I was born. Having a cop for a dad meant watching for him on TV when he was summoned to work the Thanksgiving Day Parade, getting on all the rides in Coney Island for free (back before the Knapp Commission, when cops were still "allowed to take a cup of coffee"). It meant that the kids at school snapped into attention whenever I mentioned my father's job. Meant playing with the wonderful plastic holder filled with empty .38-caliber shells after one of his mandatory afternoons killing targets on the firing range. Meant watching him clean his pistol at the dinner table whenever he was pissed off at my mother. Despite this casual approach to weapons in the household, my father—like most cops—never fired his gun outside of target practice.

The cops in my world weren't anonymous. They had faces, names, shapes, likes and dislikes. They drank Drambuie at our apartment on Sunday after-noons, showed up at the public pool from time to time in swim trunks, cursed, laughed, made mistakes, ate bologna. Some of them seemed, as the friends of one's parents so often do, to be fools. Although no newspaper-reading city girl would ever believe the police to be entirely harmless, I could see for myself that they weren't just a bunch of head-cracking animals. Occasionally unrea-sonable, occasionally stupid, yes—but not brutes.

At 18, I received a more personal education in the darker side of city law enforcement, when I got involved in an action at Washington Square Park. Instead of convincing the two officers to stop beating up the guys they were arresting, I managed to get beat up and arrested myself. With my shirt torn almost entirely off, I was handcuffed half-naked in the squad room and spent several cold and humiliating hours wondering whether I'd be raped.

I was charged with inciting a riot, assaulting an officer and resisting arrest. Next morning, a judge inspected the cuts on my face, my black eye, the bruised arms, and asked the arresting officer to describe the way in which he'd been assaulted. A Band-Aided thumb was raised in the courtroom. The cop got a lecture, the felony charges were knocked down to the catch-all misde-meanor of disorderly conduct, and I walked out of the courtroom with a sen-tence of time served. They let me off off easy, even though it didn't seem so easy at the time.

It was difficult, but not impossible, to imagine my father and his 60th Precinct friends acting like the ass-kicking Village cops who locked me up for the crime of admonishment. And it was difficult, but not impossible, to imagine the cop who beat me up going home after that shift and having supper with his wife, watching a little Johnny Carson, making jokes with his kid.

My father retired from the force around that time, and a few years later I married an ex-con. He was a predicate felon; one more strike and he would be out. Instantly, every cop on the street was a threat, and I could no longer picture them watching T.V. in some suburban family room. One single misstep or wisecrack to the wrong undercover on the wrong day might end in my husband being hauled off, shackled down, and locked away for life. I was no longer someone who viewed the cops in a positive light and generally gave them the benefit of the doubt. I was someone who mistrusted every uniform on the street, expected no mercy, expected the worst.

In 1989, two cops went out of their way to save my life. They had, under the circumstances, every reason not to, yet they broke regs for me, and because they did I am able to write these words. At the time, I was no upstanding citizen, no pillar of the community—nobody was going to get a commendation on my account. Homeless and addicted to drugs, I could have been the poster girl for a community cleanup campaign: get them off our streets! These two officers, whose names I have never learned, saw that I was barely breathing on South 2nd Street in the Williamsburg section of Brooklyn. When they couldn't get an ambulance, they threw me in the back of their squad car and raced me straight to Woodhull Hospital. It was touch-and-go for awhile, and the doctors later assured me that without the cops' quick action, there's no doubt I'd have died on that street. They saved my life in more than one way that night—this episode was the turning point that led to my current drug-free, more or less responsible life.

Today, nearly a quarter-century after my father's retirement and more than a decade since my still-unincarcerated husband and I parted ways, I find the strident, black-or-white perception of police, so common and widespread, to be as dangerous as it is false. After navigating full circle from admiration to condemnation of police and back again, I've adopted a central position that encompasses all the contradictory arcs along the way. When I was compiling this anthology, I received queries about the *police brutality* book and the *police tribute* book, as if only one or the other perspective would do. Learning that the intent of this collection was to present *all* perspectives on policing—the good, the bad, the myriad gradations of gray—many potential contributors were put off. How could it *not* be about their brutality? How could it *not* be about their sacrifice and courage?

But it is. And it is.

ANNE WALDMAN
activist, artist, teacher

WHAT THE POLICEMAN TOLD ME

the integrity of a city—any city—rests on
verbal muscle—

kill the city, insult it: again, again—

rebuild the shaven neck, the cold glint, I am
your eyes—

rebuild the *city*, I am your *cop*, I am your
gaze—

for sure I would protect the rights of those I
love—

for sure instincts are animal, jumpy—

rebuild the maneuvers for the holy homefront
state—

I jump the trigger, dragon tattoo, skull &
bones—

patriotism in fashion my flag my flag
accouterment—

bravely waves—

for sure I am scented and I am on the scent of—

I did service and I did serve—

I am loved often & well—

for sure I honor my scent and the country I
serve—

don't demonize a uniform how many there are you
will tire of—

how many serve they tire of, they never tire of—

I feel safe and never tire of—

human realm, how many are you you will tire of—

medallions, epaulets, badge for the serving
citizen you are—

for sure I will tire first, I am the first & only
policeman for you—

I carried you, I knelt down for you—

I returned for you, I covered you—

you think I am a man? is that the game—

I comforted you—

don't make assumptions about philology,
meta-texts on my beat—

shift done & shift away from me & a *gender
scent* on my beat—

cross only when you are spoken to and dare *red*,
dare *red*—

dare a language not your own—

dare it with a stick—

red lights are the contours of daring and reflex,
you'd better wait now—

outside, hands up now—

you think I like it?—

pain of the pain of the pain—

do I like it?—

call me, call one of me, one of me is ready to
pounce on Evil because I live—

I drive a flashing car & they say light the night
with optimism—

or fear?—

who do you trust?—

evil evil—

my fist through a door is powerful—

that's what I tell myself with the word *fist*
with *fear*, I say *trust*—

ambush is adrenalin in the vein although I wish
to sleep & without fear—

*herculean, plot, time, addict, money,
gun* in my little black book—

the names of some local pushers in my black
book—

they are stickfigures in movies in my tight black
book—

behind the wheel is a brute, I am his friend—

there's always a plot to not trust—

go my way for the chase?—

I misunderstood you when I did not protect you—

lights? contestatory confrontation with
inebriation—

the gangs on the street last night—

the backyard, the shattering glass—

the siren   and then it stops & goes away—

I am your every cop film—

I will never solve you for yourself—

it's a lot about identity mistaken for the
calibrated dumbshow—

that's why I speak like this—

I lifted you, I held your head, I spoke *hush*—

muttering, stuttering through troubled identity—

AUSTIN ALEXIS
adjunct professor

EYES

When I saw the cop
and he eyed me
in the dimly lit deli
his brown-eyed gaze said
I was either a criminal
or a sex object.

Later, when he spotted me
and I glimpsed him
in the neon glow
of lower Second Avenue
I felt like Marilyn Monroe:
skirt blown up, exposed,

similar to white paper
revealing intimate words.
His granite stare,
a powerful badge,
knew no dimmer,
forgot moderation.

Like an officer
in the heat of a beating,
he crouched in the furnace
of his firestorm emotion
be it animosity
or forbidden love.

DEBBIE URBANSKI
public relations artist

HOTEL, NEW YORK CITY

The night we helped put the old woman away,
the cops came and grabbed her, took all her money
while we crouched on the coldness of the bathroom floor.
She had pulled a gun out towards the end of the evening—

the cop, younger than me, touched my arm to say
girl, go back to the Midwest as fast as you can.

Her gray hair, combed wild, look familiar
outside our hotel room on the 14th floor.
Now she's spending her days locked up with the insane.
The loony bin, cops said, will do her some good.

Wait until you get, dear, everything you should—
We never figured out who exactly she screamed to.

Years ago she had been younger and pretty
with a husband and daughter who loved her enough.
Still they pushed her down stairs while she was in crutches
Killers, she yelled through the crack in our door.

This is all unfair, don't you know they murdered me?
She looked at me—green eyes—as cops led her outside.

I think of her some once I leave New York City,
and the cops' smirks when they later saw us downstairs
pushing over the front desk, demanding our money—
why'd you cause a fuss, they said, *she'd never hurt you.*

JOHN GREY
financial systems analyst

THE ARREST

Across the street,
I watch as one cop
slaps a kid against a wall,
twists his arm up
behind his back
while the other frisks him.
He's a crook,
I say to myself,
and I suddenly feel safer.
But then I think,
what if he's innocent.
And then none
of us are safe.
I walk away thinking
well as long as I'm innocent
and as long as no one
assumes I'm guilty
then I'm as safe
or as unsafe
as I was
right before I saw this incident.
As the cops drag
their suspect away,
I thank them
for clearing that up for me.

JAMES GARDNER
occupation withheld

UNTITLED

The men move like men move through a dream,
Move like men move through heavy air, a liquid
   atmosphere.
It is midnight in the projects, in the dead-end
   neighborhoods where
Worn-down Negroes move through the streets,
   contemplative and wary.
Footfall on snow is gravel shaken in a colander
    with no figure
Coincident with the sound.
In this subaqual landscape where seadrift molts
   to snowdrift
A single car circles the block. It is a bathysphere
   submerged
In this night's dark ocean and it is at the end
   of its lifeline
Where oxygen turns solid and creatures,
Evolved beyond eyes, see through their skins,
And their inverted hearts pump upward.
The car boxes the block once again and parks
   midway between the traffic light and the ambulance.
EMT's steady themselves on the seafloor ice, cross the
   littered porch into the cold hall.
The ambulance light whips through a distracted systole
   and diastole.
The windows covered in curtains and newspapers glow blood,
   then gone, with each rotation.
The snow in moonlight alternately glows
   like a hemorrhage on cotton.
Then gone. Through the door can be seen a frieze of faces
   that peer along the banister-rail,

Faces hooked by curiosity and panic,
Faces of fish that live in caves and venture out
When tragedy or the unfamiliar draws the outer world down
And in. The engine disengages. The still car waits in the street
    blocked by the ambulance with its rear doors
Swung open, empty, its low inner light, tanks, blankets folded
    and stacked, stretcher. Likewise the cruisers on the corner,
Each faces the other, each empty, dashboard and warning lights.
    The traffic signal next block distant goes yellow, then
    red, green, yellow, then red, then green, yellow. Another
    stretcher
Thrown   on the snowbank, angled upward and held in this
    foreboding tableau in which
Nothing happens. The windows mist.
The front door opens. Two cops exit. One cop sticks
His report book in his pocket. The other cop shifts
His holster belt. The two sit
In one cruiser. The beacon light goes yellow, then red, then
    green, yellow, then red. The grey exhaust follows the white snow,
    rises as slowly as the light changes. The cruiser door slams.
    It is a distant
Sudden   charge detonated. The front cruiser leaves. The rear cruiser
    tacks against the bank,
  Deep   tread catches snow, pulls away. The wipers on the parked car
    clear a crescent, cease. The scene goes incrementally
    pointillist. Two EMT's
Leave   the house, wait in the ambulance. The parked car starts,
    idles, considers, pulls without sound next to the ambulance.
    Its window
Lowers. Breath rises from the inside dark against the dashlight.
  Overdose. Overdose. Who is it. Who knows. — Is it
  Yogi on the third floor who trucks out of Brooklyn by way of
    Totowa or his wife
  Marilynn   who cadges Heineken and affection in the local spots
    or their elder son

Jonathan   who draws pictures with the caveat: "But, Mom, I don't
    always paint what you see" or their younger son
Terry   who writes poems with the self-possession of an old man
    who ruminates on baseball.
                        No.
                    Some colored girl on
    the first floor. — Dead. — Almost. — Stacy. — That's her
    name. How come. — No reason.
The ambulance attendant turns back to the dispatch radio. The car
    window
Closes.   The gone car stops at the light one block distant, its
    signal flashes red flashes red, then turns. Low reefs of plowed
    snow obscure both curbs. Grillwork and wheels protrude
    like fossils. The car motors between, under streetlight,
    stops at the next light. A woman darts
To the   window. She smiles and beckons, her mouth forms words, she
    angles towards the passenger door. The light
And the air around go green. The car pulls away. The woman floats
    for a second in the street then flees beyond the ice-drift.

God forgive our sacred hearts.

ROCHELLE RATNER
writer, critic, editor

OBJET D'ART

I thought it was just a pile of quilts and stuff, this black plastic garbage bag on this yellow quilt or piece of canvas stretched out with a couple lumps in it. Except it wasn't, it was this guy sleeping there, two quilts for a mattress, the yellow quilt covering him, his head on the garbage bag (just this drop of his head was showing. I had to get up close to make sure). And it was right near the boat basin and there was this bunch of Catholic school kids playing right there and this park police car drove on past him.

COFFEE BREAK

"I can't decide," she said.
"I understand," he said.
"I wish I could be sure," she said.

Euro-French Roast, Vanilla Hazelnut Bakery Blend, Mel's
    Neighborhood Decaf,
Sumatra Chocolate, Cappuccino, Espresso, Café Latte, Café Mocha,
    Café Con
Leche and Café Cubano

confronted them.

"Can I help you?" the server asked.
"Not yet," he said.

"How can you tell which one is the best?" she said.
"We can taste them," he said.
"We can't drink them all," she said.
"You're right," he said.

"Are you ready to order?" the server asked.
"Not yet. Serve the next person," he said.

"There's just too much to consider," she said.
"Life was easier when menus were simpler," he said.
"Maybe we should guess," she said.
"But what if we guess wrong?" he said.

"Can I help you?" the server asked again.
"No thanks. We have to go or we'll be late," he said.
"We can't decide," she said.
"I understand," the server said.

The two jurors returned to the courtroom.

STEVE DALACHINSKY

superintendent

CRIMINAL COURT

the court room is cold
today
the front row reserved for
POLICE OFFICERS AND ATTORNEYS
   ONLY

the wolf is shivering   &
i am a criminal
who trusts in god
yet finds no peace

the judge is a small jewish woman
who looks like my sister-in-law
this is not a good sign

(i know that i am guilty until proven otherwise)

we are below ground level
the windows cannot be reached
yet the wind blows
thru me
filling my stomach with
leaves.

JEANETTE CLOUGH
art researcher

JURY SELECTION

The judge asks
if I've ever had reason
to doubt the integrity of a police officer.
And out comes the whole story
about my sister on a road trip
by herself somewhere
sleeping in the car
a flashlight sluicing her face
so she rolls down a window
and the man with the badge
asks if she is all right.
She says yes.
If she is traveling alone.
She says yes.
And then, if she will give him a piece.
She answers, carefully, because he is the law
and if he decides to do it anyway
who is she, passing through with out-of-state
plates; who's around to care?
When his lights are gone she drives all night
the other direction. She does not say
what exactly happened except
he went away without getting it.
The judge asks
if she reported the incident.
I don't know, but I don't think so.
He says thank you,
and dismisses me for cause.

KIM RANSOM

youth activist

PANTOUM

The police have a description
The report just in: The Suspect—
Tall, wearing jeans, a tee-shirt and brown skin
Wanted

The report just in: The Suspect—
Channels seven, five and two
Wanted
Murdersuiciderobberyrapescandalousscandalbrownskin

Channels seven, five and two
I roll over at 6am   and hear it
Murdersuiciderobberyrapescandalousscandalbrownskin
I wonder who

I roll over at 6am   and hear it
I saw him outside my window/inside my dreams/in my kitchen eating cereal
I wonder who
"Good morning."

I saw him outside my window/inside my dreams/in my kitchen eating cereal
Tall, wearing jeans, a tee-shirt and brown skin—
"Good morning."
The police have a description

AHIMSA TIMOTEO BODHRÁN

artist, activist, academic

TARGET PRACTICE

i distinctly remember the weight of it: a big gun in my small hands at the age of four. the feel of it: shiny-silvery-smooth cold metal, n rough-ribbed black plastic. heavy, it weighed me down n scared me shitless. barely able ta hold it up, keep the barrel straight, my hands were sweaty, my ears red n throbbin, my stomach doin somersaults, cartwheels even. my eyes, as always, on the target: paper-thin black figure on a white background, pointin a similar gun back at me. *aim for the heart, mijito. aim for the heart, then pull the trigger. aim for the heart.* i always do, daddy, i always do. only the targets, only the targets have changed, papi. that, n the ammunition used.

SARAH CORTEZ
patrol police officer

ON SOME STREETS

The children don't wave
to cops. Instead, they stare
eyes glinting—an array
of hard, black diamonds.
Sallow skin. Sparse freckles.

Front-yard autos
hiked up on make-shift
stilts. A chow dog
wandering loose, patches
of fur hanging off his belly.

Each young face turning
to watch the patrol
car's path on the block.
Each face hardened
into a cold, white cipher.

ERIK LA PRADE

schoolteacher

TWO CRIMES

I

When the cops finally arrived,
They found the guy pushed
Into a corner, bleeding from
A gunshot wound. His girlfriend's
Screams filled the early morning
Darkness, waking the neighborhood.

II

One hour later,
A cop car crawled by
Searching for suspects.
I watched the car
Move out of sight,
Then turned out
The bedroom light,
Making eye contact with
My reflection in the window.

SHARON OLDS
poet & teacher

SUMMER SOLSTICE, NEW YORK CITY

By the end of the longest day of the year he could not stand it,
he went up the iron stair through the roof of the building
and over the soft, tarry surface
to the edge, put one leg over the complex green tin cornice
and said if they came a step closer that was it.
Then the huge machinery of the earth began to work for his life,
the cops came in their suits blue-grey as the sky on a cloudy evening,
and one put on a bullet-proof vest, a
black shell around his own life,
life of his children's father, in case
the man was armed, and one, slung with a
rope like the sign of his bounden duty,
came up out of a hole in the top of the neighboring building
like the gold hole they say is in the top of the head,
and began to lurk toward the man who wanted to die.
The tallest cop approached him directly,
softly, slowly, talking to him, talking, talking,
while the man's leg hung over the lip of the next world
and the crowd gathered in the street, silent, and the
hairy net with its implacable grid was
unfolded near the curb and spread out and
stretched as the sheet is prepared to receive at a birth.
Then they all came a little closer
where he squatted next to his death, his shirt
glowing its milky glow like something
growing in a dish at night in the dark in a lab and then
everything stopped
as his body jerked and he
stepped down from the parapet and went toward them
and they closed on him, I thought they were going to
beat him up, as a mother whose child has been
lost may scream at the child when it's found, they

took him by the arms and held him up and
leaned him against the wall of the chimney and the
tall cop lit a cigarette
in his own mouth, and gave it to him, and
then they all lit cigarettes, and the
red, glowing ends burned like the
tiny campfires we lit at night
back at the beginning of the world.

TONY GLOEGGLER
group home manager

GRAVEYARD SHIFT

He leans back
in his leather lounge chair,
drinks a cold Michelob, aims
the remote at the T.V.
Click. Channel 16.
The Knicks-Sixers game.
Nothing but a bunch of monkeys
jumping up and down the court.
He flicks the switch.
Channel 7. Eyewitness News
shows a march through Bensonhurst.
Whites line the streets, spit
watermelon seeds, chant

NIGGERS GO HOME
NIGGERS GO HOME

His fingers find the beat, drum
the armrest in time. Al Sharpton
steps to the microphone, starts
to speak.
        He grits his teeth,
mumbles, "Shut the fuck up"
and squeezes the OFF button.
The screen flashes gray, swallows
that fat black face in one big gulp.
He finishes his beer, goes
upstairs to shower, and comes down
smelling of Brut, dressed in blue.
Strapping a belt around his waist,
he places the .38 in its holster,
picks up his night stick,
walks out the door.

LOGIC OF FATE

Mayor Giuliani,

The world has a logic.

If your cops
shoot enough (unarmed)
black men,

the KKK
will march
in Manhattan

the same way
if a band plays music
someone will dance.

JACKIE SHEELER
copdaughter, dayjobholder

CRAYOLA WARS

The color of the body
has begged the beginning
of a million murderous

scenes. I would never be
shot down 41 times in some hallway
by men with eyes as blue

as my own handsome cop-daddy's eyes
because my body is the color of protection.
Every day I strut past the target-practice hearts of the police

holding court on the street, and I'm never afraid.
I have lived among badges all my life
growing numb, going blind to the uniforms.

Darken me into cowardice, then:
tan me black, fill
in between my lines with Burnt Sienna

the best of all those good Crayola names
the blackest of the browns
more certain than Raw Umber to result

in frequent frisks and eventual capture
in this grown-up game of cops and maybe robbers
where the cap guns always malfunction

and bang bang you're dead
is written in blood the color of tenement brick
drying on the stoops of certain neighbors.

NAT READ
LAPD

YOU AND ME, CHARLIE (EXCERPT)

The legislator's asleep
And so are The People who elected him.
I'm the one they paid to stay awake tonight
And carry out the laws they felt like passing.
It's just you and me out here, Charlie.
And you're going to jail.

JOHN PAUL DAVIS
bike messenger

(WTO FREEWRITE)

lines composed a couple thousand miles away from seattle, where cops with guns protect big business from protestors with dangerous placards.

network news is a nightmare i'm forced to watch every night,
trapped between five and five-thirty.

in seattle, cops link together, an exoskeleton,
a hard machine of boots & visors & riot shields,
a hive-mind buzzing walkie-talkie code,
a barbed-wire spine, the stiff flesh of fists.

martial law means concentration camps are okay.

hey man, they're just doing their jobs,
says a guy on the news.
no one told him
somebody had to buy them all that riot gear.
somebody put duct-tape x's on the sidewalk telling the police where to
     line up.

being a cop means never having to say you're sorry.

i want to carry a sign for a good cause
so i can learn why some instinct
like a hot nerve with the insulation peeled back
won't let me believe that cops are the good guys.

it'd be a rough school, for sure,
bony knee press my neck to asphalt,
the spicing of my skin with pepper spray,
then meat-tenderizing nightsticks,
the shucking away of each constitutional right
until i'm ready to be cooked in court.

rights are things you're allowed to have until you need them.

i want to be strip-searched, so i can learn
the government's precise language of violation,
so i can feel like an underdeveloped nation
in the barbiturate arms of the world trade organization.

i could let the surgical hands sweep over me,
dive into me. i would hire a lawyer
so i'd know the distinct pleasure
of not being allowed to call him.

i pay taxes
so the government can hire cops
to haul me away should i refuse
to pay taxes.

martial law means they can jail you for thinking.

an otherwise noble man i know says he votes
republican because i don't want anyone
to take away my stuff.

in seattle, there's an alien landscape
of lingering tear gas, each wet particle
illuminated by the holy aura
of t.v. spotlights. transmitters throbbing
video signals up to satellites, to sell
us the idea that policemen are heroes.

on t.v., corporations are called "advertisers."
in congress, they're called "lobbyists."
the fraternal order of police calls them "distinguished donors."

police brutality is a noun edited out of news bulletins.

on-the-scene reporters wait while cops
crawl on their bellies through smoke
to beat their chests, make vulture noises, & declare
on national t.v.,
"we're not here to protect the people,
we're here to protect the property."

on the day
they were passing out brains to countries,
god ran out & all america
got was a network.

martial law means they can jail you for turning off the t.v.

PATRICK SEGUIN

copywriter

DALHOUSIE

Walking the streets with a great deal of concern and consternation;
Who will be the challenger tonight?
Jumping into the fray unschooled and ill-equipped,
You wear that navy well, sir,
And the schoolgirls are crazy about that shady important hat.

The lights rotate
Up and down Dalhousie,
Where the stupid chickenfish women dance, bleed and die
At the hands of their arrogant agents and violent clients.

This beat is full of the same shit and feeble hopes.
You know they can escape;
By helping them, you become the enemy, their guilty savior.
Those crisp creases and that lickable badge,
And the schoolboys are mad about that shady important hat.

There's a tangible quality in the air,
It tastes like lipstick, blood, lubricant, cheap wine,
Smoke, urine, dirty skin and more lipstick.

Skulls will be cracked tonight.
Wrists will be scraped and bruised.
Mercy will be subtle and not without some pain.

But you love them.
In some arcane way
You really love them.

JOHN B. LEE
poet, editor, teacher

RUMOURS OF POLICE

On our first night in Johannesburg
there is a sudden commotion
in the parking lot
just outside of the well-glassed restaurant
where we are, with our calamari
and Windhock beer
simply beginning our visit

and there just beyond the circle of light
tossing its thin silk in a yellow drift
of its own description
just there by the car in question
sitting in shadow
like something sunk to the roof line in brackish water
while five youths scatter
as the illuminating blue swirl of the law arrives
and we watch it all
like cockroach scuttle
as one constable, his hands lamping the tree
becomes someone simply sweeping the dark
from the limbs of a larch...

and there is nothing there
nothing to satisfy or disappoint
nothing to drag by the leg

and as we watch
the policemen go
and after in the slowing
those who have run away
return

to surround the little car
glancing up as if a kite were caught
and tearing its own cloth in the grief.

And so, our conversation
turns to intersections to avoid
for fear of guns
to why we must never stop at stoplights
to how a husband was shot in his home
to carjackings, to drugs
and the crime
of those in a hurry to be
'not poor'
'not homeless' 'not jobless'
'not without water' 'not
without food'   'not here'
our conversation turns
in candle flame
and white wine flavour
and in the good cheer of linguini con mari
to where, outside the window
those city children
mill around that car in question
looking up
and wondering
what's up there in the branches?
how might it set us free?

ROBIN BETH SCHAER
graduate student

HIDING PLACE

I hold his knife beneath my breast, inside
my bra's elastic, on nights Irish cops
are out in heavy uniforms, too hot
for summer, gripping their nightsticks. I hide

the knife where they won't look. They'd arrest him
if they could, just for being with me,
not his own kind. The strange weight makes me lean
over, crooked, as we make our way home.

I tell him it's slipping. Come here, he says,
pulling me close in a fake embrace
to hide his thumb pushing it back in place.
Upstairs, I drop it by our bed, undress.

His lips tug at my skin, until his head
goes soft, rolls quietly beneath my breast.

JANELL MOON
hypnotherapist, workshop leader

FOUND POEM
composed from a KQED radio broadcast

"Help me, help me. He's gonna kill me.
I know he's gonna kill me.
Help, help me, quick. He's at me again.
Ohhh…"

"Bitch. What you doing? Get off that phone."

"Hello. What's wrong. Who's that in the background.
Hello. Answer me."

"Never mind. I'm sorry I called. I shouldn't have called."

"Ma'am, where are you? What's your name? Who's with you?"

"It's just me throwing a fit. I shouldn't have called.
Please, please. I shouldn't have called."

"Ma'am, we don't want you to get hurt. Are you okay?"

"Yeah, I'm fine. I'm just throwing a tantrum.
Don't come, okay? Everything is fine."

"We've traced the call. We know where you are. If you don't
want us to come, say a number between 1 and 5."

"Six."

RICHARD WILMARTH
guitarist

CHARLES F. KELLEY

i thought of my grandfather
    when i reported my car stolen
        at the providence, rhode island police station
because my grandfather was a policeman
    in nearby fall river, massachusetts
and he used to take me to the front desk
    when i was a little boy to show me off
        to all of his friends who were on duty
and now the thoughts of my grandfather
    are coming back to me again tonight
        while reporting my car stolen
    in the providence, rhode island police station
thinking of him dead
    for over 35 years
and me standing there talking to the desk sergeant
    who reminds me of my grandfather
        who died of cancer in his mid-fifties
as i remember his alcoholism
remember him taking me to the lock-ups
remember him taking me to the statue of liberty
remember him attending every world series
remember him in the hospital dying
feeling his life becoming my own
but not believing it until tonight
when i had to see the world as it really is
and not through a little boy's eyes

MARJ HAHNE
educator

FATHER: A LIFE IN BLUE COUNTS

Harlem beat
wife at home in dress
night shift

nab
a purse snatcher
name on brass plate

cop of the month
scotch & water after work
      '64 Chevelle rams neighbor's fence

plain clothes
the mob in Bedford-Stuy
sheepwolfsheep

28 and 26
kids and 3 kids later
kindergarten next fall

NYPD blue
moves to suburb to co-own a Sunoco
collar blues bluer

found
love letter in glove compartment
"Mud" or move

fixer-upper
weekend builder
home wrecker

auto mechanic
my dad's tougher than yours
he was a cop in Harlem

20 years
coulda had a pension
doing time

job
after job after
job

42
hourly wage / no medical
collecting regrets

found
Valentine boxers in VW trunk
family therapy

married up
sins of the father
passed down

son leaves
one daughter starves
other daughter rages

forgive
forgive
forgive

65
scrape calcified backbone
return beneath the cars

MY BROTHER, A COP

You are a cop, which still surprises me from time
to time. After all, I knew you as a preemie runt,
wrinkled and red skinned, crying, screaming,
in the incubator. You were on your back, your arms
wide and outstretched, your knees bent and your legs
thin. Veins and light could be seen through areas
of your body. Like me, you were tiny and your survival
at birth, uncertain. I went to the hospital gift shop to buy
your first toy, a '59 Chevy sedan. Like me, you like cars.

You are a cop, recently made Sergeant. The first time
you declined so you could be home with your growing
children, and gained respect from many. Once, years ago
you drove me through your precinct. Gutted buildings,
littered lots where houses once stood, burglar bars on
corner stores. Liquor stores and storefront Baptist
churches. Some waved, others greeted. It was real
not fake, not smiles for The Man. I knew you were a
good cop. You've done 18 years now and never once
have shot a man, a woman, a child. Once, I heard you
say to a photographer, "Those people don't have much
and I will not take you to stick a camera in their faces."
You could have been reprimanded. Instead, he said,
"I understand." As a teenager, you liked Eastwood's
Dirty Harry movies. You liked his courage for truth
and duty. His disdain for petty bureaucrats
and self-serving politicians. Before him, you
admired John Lennon. You cried when he was
murdered. You always were alive to pain, and cared.

WILLIAM F. RUTKOWSKI

instrument maker

FALL OF NINETY

In the fall of ninety,
in a small-town cop bar with my brother the small-town cop.
We pass the time with his cohort.
He is a young Ajax strong in battle.

The old tales are told:
How in the county jail he toughed it as point man on the goon squad—
broke the riot and some heads.
How he bridled this big townie with his nightstick and rode him down like
a bronco as he tried to run.
How he tired of talk and just lost it on some swinging drunk.

The one story I tell:
How he breathed and beat life back into a dying neighbor,
They don't follow and return to the recount of knockdowns.
Silent my young brother just nods his head.

And I barely can recall many falls ago,
When a small boy beagled the coming cold,
smiled and said how much the world smelled
like Halloween.

JACK ANDERSON
poet & dance critic

IN UNIFORM

The other night in a bar
where guys can come as they wish
I met this cop.

At least he said he was a cop
and he was dressed like a cop—
well, sort of.

He said he'd never wear
a real uniform to a bar
lest the guys think it a raid.

So he prefers to look coplike
in a costume not a uniform
that's still his uniform for the bars at night.

And because he wore that costume
and not a regulation uniform
I could relax with him there.

He wants to have me up to his apartment sometime:
if I go, what I'll find him as I cannot imagine
nor will I know what I'll be until we decide on it.

CHRISTINA WOŠ DONNELLY

writer, mother

ON MY WAY TO THE POETRY SLAM

So I'm halfway down the off-ramp,
and the siren and the flashing lights
startle me.
And, as I'm pulling over,
I'm thinking, "What now?"
and "Damn! I'll be late."
and "Well, so what?"
And then I take a good, deep breath
and before I can re-open my eyes,
I hear this roar from behind me,
"Pull farther right."
and so I do, and as I remember
that I ate off all my lipstick, I hear
another roar, "Have your license ready."
And so I do, but I'm wondering
if I just reach in again
to get my lipstick,
will he think I'm going for a gun?
And while I'm trying to weigh
which is worse, to be seen
by a stranger, without lipstick,
or find myself looking up the barrel
of his gun, he startles me again
by yelling something,
I don't remember what,
right through the window,
which I roll down and say,
in genuine bewilderment,
"Did I do something wrong?"
And, get this, he leans his whole arm
against my car and practically leers
and says, "Well, I'm not sure."
To which, I can think of

no response whatsoever.
And then he straightens up and scowls,
 "You were clocked going 74,"
which I know is so not true,
because I was there.
So I say, "No, I don't think so.
I never speed."
And then he says, "Oh, well,
I wasn't sure. I was chasing
a red car, but I lost sight of it,
and I saw you pulling onto the ramp,
and that's usually what they do,
they pull off, onto the ramp.
So I chased you, but then
as you're pulling over,
I'm thinking to myself,
'Maybe that car was a darker red.'
And then you say,
'Was I doing something wrong?'
So, it's your lucky day.
You're free to go," but he's still
standing there. So I say,
"OK.
Listen, is it going to upset you
if I put on my lipstick?" And he says,
"Not at all." So I reach in and get it,
but then
I start weighing which is worse
to keep sitting there without lipstick
or put it on in front of a man
with a demonstrated history of leering,
so I just hold it in my hand
while he apologizes, "Sorry
to hold you up." And I say,
"That's all right." And he's still
standing there. So I say,
"I never speed.

My reflexes are kind of slow,
so I usually hover
just under the speed limit
and annoy people that way."
And he says, "Well, have a good night."
and "Be careful pulling out."
So he leaves, finally,
and I take another deep breath
and put on my lipstick, and
look carefully pulling out, and
here I am. So that's why
I was almost late
and why I might've been
shaking a little.
It was so surreal.

Do I need more lipstick?

RALPH POMEROY
art critic & lecturer

CORNER

The cop slumps alertly on his motorcycle,
supported by one leg like a leather stork.
His glance accuses me of loitering.
I can see his eyes moving like fish
in the green depths of his green goggles.

His ease is fake. I can tell.
My ease is fake. And he can tell.
The fingers armored by his gloves
splay and clench, itching to change something.

As if he were my enemy or my death,
I just stand there watching.

I spit out my gum which has gone stale.
I knock out a new cigarette—
which is my bravery.
It is all imperceptible:
The way I shift my weight,
the way he creaks in his saddle.

The traffic is specific though constant.
The sun surrounds me, divides the street between us.
His crash helmet is whiter in the shade.
It is like a bull ring as they say it is just
    before the fighting.
I cannot back down. I am there.

Everything holds me back.
I am in danger of disappearing into the sunny dust.
My levis bake and my T-shirt sweats.

My cigarette makes my eyes burn.
But I don't dare drop it.

Who made him my enemy?
Prince of coolness. King of fear.
Why do I lean here waiting?
Why does he lounge there watching?

I am becoming sunlight.
My hair is on fire. My boots run like tar.
I am hung-up by the bright air.

Something breaks through all of a sudden,
and he blasts off, quick as a craver,
one with his power; watching me watch.

RYN GARGULINSKI

journalist

THE SPECTACLE

you always have to push it
my boyfriend said as
the two no-longer undercover cops wrote out the
tickets and the
beer swirled down the platform drain and I
cursed myself for being stupid.

had to be a smart ass.

holding my boyfriend's beer while he tied his shoe
proved fatal when I took
the two bottles in bags—one in each hand—and
pretended to be drunk and
wobbly calling undue attention to myself holding the
two open bottles
ill-concealed to begin with—one in each hand—
making funny faces
holding them
high
over my head making funny faces slurring words
saying something like
I'm really drunk hee-a-haw
even though I wasn't.

had to be a clown.

a train rushes by.
I look at the summons.
$50.
shit.

a train rushes by.
he doesn't look at the summons.
stuffs it in his
jean jacket pocket.

as the cops
walk away
they say
we were going
to let
it go.

SUSAN KATZ
new media poet

5XPLUS

my husband
has a big mouth.
when he's drunk
it gets coarser.
i have signed
5 complaints; they're
stuffed in the bottom
of my bag
hidden
(that does not include
the time
i was surrounded
by police
in front of
my apt. build
ing and an ambulance
came to take me
to Bellevue
for 5 weeks incarcer
ation, inciner
ation).
and, as is
his temper
ament,
i received 3
visits
from him
in 5 weeks.
So, when he was
arrested for
harassment
of our ex-lawyer's
'significant other'

i accompanied him
to the 17th precinct
to see
his pockets
emptied
to see
him sweat
while he waited
on Yom Kippur
for a computer
printout
of his past.

DOROTHY BATES

editor, lyricist, poet

THE GREAT FLOWER BUST

In the city, every springtime,
an ancient troll from Jersey
(without benefit of permit)
sold flowers on my corner,
just picked and country cheap.

I arrived, that fatal April,
cash in hand, to find
a large police pick-up,
rear-end enclosed in wire,
all the flowers thrown inside.
Two cops, their duty done,
drove them away.

They had arrested the flowers.

Anemones apprehended!
Bluebells behind bars!

I figured the roses
and tulips would be
the first to go.
Then, drooping,
dropping, and D.O.A.,
all the rest.

The cactus plants, however,
tough as street kids,
would draw a little blood
before they died.

MIKE WILSON
attorney

UNTITLED

Perpetrator caught—
    policeman in the mirror,
victim in his arms.

HOWARD PFLANZER
playwright

TOMPKINS SQUARE PARK, MAY 1, 1990

Lights out in the bandshell
A cop struck by a bottle
Thrown from the crowd.

Other cops panic
Near riot
Many injured
Many arrested.

A war zone
Along A
Helmeted troops
Blocking 9th
Scanning passersby with
Razor sharp eyes
Ready to slash them
Neatly
To prepare them
Bleeding
For display
On the white sheets
In the waiting vans.

Back in the park
Squatters chanting
Waving red flags
Adorned with black circles
Cut through by lightning bolts
Beginning with crosses
Ending with arrows.

Sudden shouts
People running
Someone raises
An American flag
Then burns it.

The smell of smoke
Fills the spring air
As two men
With camcorders
Video the event.

Though I am not a camera
The park on a spring night
Is caught in my memory.

SUSAN MAURER
social worker

POLICE BLOTTER

I search the hieroglyph on the sand
The gull's X, the tire rune, the sneaker tread
Some differing bare feet, the small cloven hoof prints
From a deer
My friend hates them
"Bang, bang Bambi," she says
We observe them, disguised as workmen
Trying to fool us
It doesn't work

I have come to the sea to be baptized
I go in and come back, chastened, wet only to the knees
Not like Aimee Semple McPherson
Who died that way
I'll try again tomorrow
For baptism, I mean, or do I mean christening

The phone wakes me
My friend tells the police
A small stag is tangled in her hammock
By his horns

"Aha," I say, "your deer trap worked"
She is not amused and leaves me to deal
With my coffee and the police

When they come
They wear tight jeans and are cute
I fumble for the towel they ask me for
While they joke around me
I drink my coffee and do not look
I hear the thrashing in the brush

And it's done
Towel over deer's eyes
They tell me and hammock cut
And off he goes wearing a crown of string

The police want my name and birth date
Do they need my birth date? I give them my birth date
They give me the pink towel, unharmed

In high season this would be headline news
On the police blotter section
Of The Fire Island Times
This is my report

That evening I see deer on the beach
About four of them
They walk from pile of seaweed to pile of seaweed
Sniffing with startled disdain
Everything is greyed slightly in the sunset
Except the sun and streaks of cloud of peach
I walk in again up to my knees
Tomorrow is another day

DEER PRUDENCE

We were dressed in red as children, bright
as bloody angels on christmas trees,
the dogs stuffed like sausages into
humiliating neon dog sweaters.

My mother explained that
there were hunters who came and shot
the deer that lived in back of our house
and I asked why they
shot the deer and she said
to eat them and I asked why
we had to wear red and she said
so we didn't get shot.

This is how I learned that there are men who would gladly
tie a small child to the roof of their car
mount its head on the wall, separate
the corpse into ribs, stew and roast
pour a snifter of something not as dark as blood, say
Honey, look what I got.
I saw living rooms with little stuffed kid heads on the wall,
little stuffed kid heads with glazed, glassy eyes.

I have been wearing a red sweater
every day for a month now.
I stand dumb and shocked as a deer in
headlights watching frozen as
after breakfast she wanders
into his field and the silent shot, the rock of the
fist of a stranger cold cocks her, point blank range.

She is sitting in a chair and the clean blue cops stand
around her, tall like buildings, and

tell her it's a jungle out there she
should really be more careful.
She holds a cold cloth to her eye
covering the blood spot inside that glares
like a bullseye moved off its target.

Later, I spill my heart like vomit
blueberries and blood and the other thing
besides her glasses that was shattered:
that I did nothing

that I could do nothing;
but she says, you did, you jumped
at him, yelling, like a, like an
animal protecting its young or something but
I don't remember it so it didn't happen.

A hunter knows very little about a deer
except the way its head tips to eat or drink
the way it holds itself in the bush.
The rest is chance and the cruelty of time and
location and I'd like to say I
crept through the mission, dangling silver change
like a lure, wearing my body like
a six-foot salt lick but
the fact was I was smoking cigarettes
to make the bus come.

I saw him before he spoke to me.
I recognized the way he moved from up the street
erratic and wary and
tight inside his clothes
moving in small explosions and sidling up to strangers
checking the fit of his cross-hairs
and he slid up alongside me
his glazed eyes at the ground
his hands coils of anger, clenching at each soft word

got any change
and still struggling to get my head through the
red dog sweater I grabbed by mistake
I poke my elbow through
the neck instead of the arm and shaking I
hand him my last quarter since 9-1-1 is free and
the cops come slow as love with their clean blue suits and
clean black guns and he was
cornered in the alley
trussed up in handcuffs
strapped on their hood and then, sealed safely back inside,
they drove away in their clean, clean car and
I'm almost at the point where I can joke that
that buck stopped there but when I shut
my eyes he is hanging there, washed, combed and stuffed,
eyes harder than trophy plaque wood
eyes wet as wounds
locked in mine
at point blank range.

GIL FAGIANI
social work administrator

SWEET STREAMS
IN SPANISH HARLEM

The snow cone seller's
wooden cart
lies on its side
along Third Avenue
its shiny turquoise paint
showing the footprint
of the cop
who kicked it over
for unregulated
business practice

Out of the mouths
of broken bottles
syrupy streams
of purple, green and orange
inch their way
across the sidewalk
towards the Coloso
Furniture Store
where beds collapse
upon human contact

HALLOWEEN

it is the end
October in its reds and yellows
and Billy Last Crow is passing
through this town like a ghost
boots knocking the sidewalk

if this town were somewhere else
the police would stop him
for not belonging

nice neighborhood

it is the end of the day
and children are coming outside
dressed as the latest cultural myths
WWF gods and japanese anime stars
walking past the SUVs
and other luxury cars

on a telephone wire
a raven stares Edgar Allan
at Billy striding by
as the sun gutters he steps
into a crosswalk thinking this might be
his last night

his feet hurt from the miles
for a moment he doesn't know
what state this is
rattlers in his stomach as the first
police car rolls into view

a drifting indian is a ghost in this world
or he becomes one soon enough
out of instinct
Billy Last Crow drops his eyes
to his boots avoiding looking at

the houses
the cars
the kids
the cops
and he walks a little faster
mutters a new old indian prayer

get my ass out of here

he feels the cops staring at him
as they drive by slowly
in another town
they would have just pulled
up along side
they would have had him spread
eagle on the hot engine hood
straps to their revolvers undone
and waiting for him to speak up
to say something Sitting Bull
or Crazy Horse

Billy prays for fast legs
and invisibility
he doesn't look back at them
knows they are back there
watching his long hair swaying
he sees a group of kids
on the sidewalk before him

little *spidermen* and *austin powers*
laughing and talking loud
a princess or fairy
the suspicious eye of a cross
armed parent
and a little fellow 4 years old
wearing hollywood indian skins

this crazy world
being what you are
can get you killed
and to be something
untrue unreal
will get you candy

SHERYL L. NELMS
insurance investigator

IF LOOKS COULD

I try to look him in the eyes

but can't

he has perfected it

the icy stare
comes
from the bottom
of his brown eyes

says it's a habit
learned it over
in Arkansas
when he was police chief

says he used it
and his uniform
for crowd control

when Wallace was running

ANDRES CASTRO
small press founder/editor

CONFLUENCE BECOMES ME

I

In this Queens neighborhood late one night in '64 Kitty Genovese was repeatedly stabbed until dead, while thirty-eight neighbors came to their windows without calling police (strange for a white middle class neighborhood it was thought). A social-psychological phenomena researchers said: "the large number of witnesses diffused responsibility."

II

I moved to Kew Gardens in '82, to a building without a single black or Latino. My wife, Japanese (a more acceptable minority some say), was screened by the landlord—I was a later surprise. But you know, I looked Italian, he said, "and since you're newlyweds this small apartment would only be good for a year or two, right?" The landlord soon died of a heart attack: seems too quick losing fifty pounds on a liquid protein diet. The building went to an agency that hired a Mexican super who then screened for tenants. Soon after, a Punjabi bought the place: needless to say, more color-filled every year. White flight, and old-timer death continues.

III

Now it's no secret some crazy cops in New York City love to kill some young men—especially of color, especially when slow to bow. And a good number of neighbors say these tactics work: murder rate lowest since the 60's. Some say nothing keeps us more in place than lots of new prisons. How many angels can dance on the thread between cause and effect?

IV

Around midnight a screeching car, then screams, pull me to my third floor window: two white cops chasing a young black man, with little hope of catching him until one yells, "Stop or I'll shoot." He stops, and drops to the ground. And they start barking, "Put your hands behind your back!" Whirling batons and maniacal kicks plow into his legs and torso. He doesn't have a chance. I wonder what he did. As I push up on my window a neighbor yells out, "Hey, what's going on out there?" The black man screams back, "They're killing me! They're killing me! Somebody help me!" One cop suddenly straightens, and stops kicking, as if someone had called him by name. The other digs one last heel into the sprawled figure's back, and then slips a baton under his neck. In a chokehold, and cuffed, he's brought gasping and wobbling to his feet. They both throw him head first against the squad car hood and quickly shove him in the back seat. Seconds after the back door slams the car speeds away, and sharply rounds the corner.

V

My eyes move back to the beating as if it were a looping movie scene. There he is again, his face pressed into the sidewalk. The brutal pounding of baton blows to the back, arms, and cuffed hands. Screams of, "Here, here, take my hands! I'm not fighting. Take my hands!" The cops yelling over him "Don't move! Give me your hands!" I hear my neighbor's window come down. It's late. I need to go to work tomorrow.

VI

Someone made Genovese's attacker stop and run away by yelling from their window, but cops were still not called, and moments later that psychopath returned to finish her in a doorway. Diffusion of responsibility in Kitty's case meant nearly forty witnesses assumed or hoped someone else would call police.

VII

Looking out from my window one last time, the sidewalk grows hazy; strangely, I see myself inside the Austin Street Ale House, sitting across from two large freckled cops—and their muttering about fuckin faggots and Spiks stinkin up The Dept. How enjoyable to see that the more calmly I sit looking over my New York Times, the more I savor each sip of my Glenfiddich, the louder they become, the meaner their glares. At my age, in my beard and brown summer skin I've never been more Puerto Rican, or American. And I don't know whether I thought of it then, or I'm thinking of it now, but Kitty was murdered just a few doorways down from where we all sat drinking.

VICTIMS & PERPETRATORS

The victim, found in the basement of a seven-story building, is in guarded condition at Central Hospital. The perpetrators were arrested at the scene.

The victim testified before a grand jury yesterday afternoon; three of the five perpetrators remain at large.

Victims, potential victims—"vics" in the offhand lingo of street felons—are, we think, a recognizable class. Stripped of valuables, swaddled in gauze, shoveled into the backs of speeding ambulances or outlined in chalk on the street, oh yes, we know exactly who they are. The victim is never feared, of course; we only fear becoming one ourselves.

Perpetrators creep across the world free and invisible until—and sometimes even during—the moment of commission. Suspected perps, identified (or misidentified) by neighborhood, skin color, gang stripe or demeanor, are herded into lineups, labeled as suspects until a trembling finger points and a testifying mouth shapes the sentence. "He's the one." "That's her." "It was them." "Those two right there."

We never use these words to describe the police: those blue-suited intermediaries, brokering the grim world between victim and perpetrator: rescuing the one, apprehending the other, taking copious if cryptic notes all the while. Just doing their job.

But what if the job is "doing" them? When most waking hours are spent in a repetitive grid of blood and weapons, rescues and executions, accidents and incidents, how is a person changed? Does the constant act of impersonally recording the stream of human tragedy result in the depersonalization of humanity itself? Or, conversely, result in a skewed view of the world where anything that is not tragedy can no longer be perceived?

The two groups of poems in *Victims & Perpetrators* allow the police to inhabit those unfamiliar roles: not as enforcers outside looking in, taking action, making notes, but as victims of a brutal job or perpetrators of brutality within the context of that job. One goes inevitably, if reluctantly, with the other.

When young men went to Vietnam in the 1960's to fight an extended hand-to-hand/face-to-face war, they were indelibly altered by their time in the jungle. Those who coped by out-bruting the brutes and skewering Asian babies on their GI bayonets would never have learned these dark skills back home in Minneapolis or Boston; likewise, the men who returned asweat with fear, consumed by nightmare, unable to assume the mantle of everyday American life were also responding to the conditions in which they had been placed. In each case the changes were too often irrevocable and complete.

True, Des Moines is not Hanoi, and San Francisco is no Saigon. But for thousands of cops patrolling the urban core of cities like Los Angeles, New York, Detroit, Miami, New Orleans and Chicago, the risks and the fear and the routinization of murder have placed them into something very much like a war zone—where they measure their service in decades, not months or years.

What is fermenting in the vast American laboratory of the streets?

VICTIMS

TIFF HOLLAND
dispatcher, copwife

NIGHT SHIFT ON THE POISONOUS WORLD

Midnight shift at the P.D.,
passing around photos of the dead,
those who died under suspicious circumstances—morgue
photos with blood-draining tubes from the noses,
documenting the surreal, multicolor
spectrum of blood-settling bruises,
aching beyond the capacity for pain.

Nude photos of the sexless dead:
"thirty-year-old white female, alcoholic"—
looking like no thirty year old I've ever
seen, no woman, her organs
no longer containing appropriate fluids,
blood filling the body cavity.

A Polaroid,
"fifty-two-year-old male,"
not missed, by the living,
for nine days. The officers
taking the DOA

had to call for cigars, and purposely
burned coffee while snapping these shots.
He was found, naked
with a plastic bag pulled over
his head and a shoestring,
bow tied around his neck,
the gift wrap straining by the ninth
day to contain his death-bloated face.

At the nine-one-one seminar
for beginning dispatchers we're taught
men often strip to take their lives.
Women are more likely to go to
motels, not wanting to make
a mess at home. Males, more
territorial, want to leave their mark.

The fifty-two-year-old
in the Polaroid had wedged a screwdriver into
the garage door to prevent any entry,
any escape, except, after
the ninth day, the smell.

He came in a nuisance call—
the neighbors complaining, he must
not have taken out his trash.
Tomorrow would have been his birthday.

I am reading Delmore Schwarz between calls,
"the poisonous world flows into my mouth
    like water into a drowning man's."
One of the cops, passing around the photos,
tells me about the morgue.
"Amazing," he says, "you have to learn
    to throw the bodies around like dolls
    to work there,
    you have to."

PAT FALK
english professor

ROOKIE

I don't remember the dead boy's name,
the clothing he was wearing
or the street—neon or darkness,
there must have been
a stir or sound, the wind perhaps,
or the humming of the crowd.

Vaguely a river of blood,
moving past the storefront down
the sidewalk, a small black pool
gathered at the curb—and the pen
in my hand, writing, *two in the head
and his neck was slashed.*

I know only the rhythm of detail,
syncopation in a field report,
something to dance to,
a fever of sorts. *Two in the head
and his neck a river,* faces gathered
white with rage—watching.

ROSS MARTIN

...is guilty

THE COP WHO RIDES ALONE

passes rendezvous
in the park
and thinks about

parking, bores of
traffic
too easily

may
or may not
listen to self-

help tapes
considers getting a dog
calls for

backup
but never bleeds.
The cop who rides alone

is or appears to be
tougher
than the cop who needs

a partner
buddy with a matching
holster

a man to kick in doors for
with a comparably shiny
badge

a man to take
turns driving with
or bleed to

death on
whose eyes can't
heal but like saturated

tourniquets
do their best.

J.J. CAMP

police officer

INSIDE

(a consideration of my police car, maybe its driver)

I've had ten, maybe
a dozen in two dozen
years of this work. Mostly,
they're the same steel
framed gas-drinking four wheels
and someone to steer—
toward danger, not love.
Radio shoots complaints at me.
No vest protects.
Switches: radio, siren, lights
all worn smooth
by my repeated touch.
Grit along the dashboard
Smell of coffee spilled
outdone by pungent
dog shit tracked in on my boot.
Once bright interior has faded
to some nondescript
other. I lose
that will to do I once possessed.
It has leaked out
slowly from unseen
holes.

There's competition
for memory's place
in the car with me:
The boy—finger torn away,
as I race his blood
to see who's fastest.
The young man's body,
black from hours in the flames
he lit himself.
(But what about his wife?)
The girl before me,
far from love, hesitation
scarred from elbow to wrist,
one breath from suicide
now.

Anticipation:
a million breathless
possibilities blind
my overactive
maybe-oriented
never-too-careful
sense of real possibilities,
like black
bands hiding other cops' badges.
(Someone cries quietly.)
The long wait:
an unanswered
knock at three AM
the distant phone rings
in desperation, wanting
just one word.

MAGGIE DUBRIS
paramedic, writer, musician

WILLIEWORLD (EXCERPT)

They say that it takes time for things to change, but this is a lie. Change is analogous to a bolt of lightning. Instantaneous. The way your clothes turn into laundry when you take them off and throw them in the hamper. One minute you're doing the dishes, then a bubble bursts inside your skull and you're lying on the floor biting your tongue off. God sets his tiny time bombs, and you are there when they explode.

The first time I came in contact with the killer of one of my patients was uptown, in a block of renovated brownstones in Harlem. The family owned the whole building. In the first floor bedroom a black man in his nineties was kneeling on the floor, slumped against the side of the bed. He was clutching a scarf, and had been stabbed eight or nine times in the chest. You wouldn't think that somebody could die in that position, but he was already beginning to get stiff. When I went into the kitchen to get the information, the police had the person who had killed him handcuffed to the table. It was a junkie; a very small woman who could have been anywhere from eighteen to forty. Her arms and neck were all keloid scars from shooting up, and I thought she must live in the streets because she was so dirty. The man's son had come home from church and caught her leaving the building. When he took her inside he found his father's body. She had stolen only a pair of brass cufflinks and some dress shirts that were still wrapped in cellophane. The old man had bought them the morning before. The son kept pounding his fist into the wall, but he never hit the junkie; just tied her up until the police got there. The junkie didn't seem human to me. She was at the kitchen table, giving everybody dirty looks and yelling at the cops that they were racists because they wouldn't take the handcuffs off her. The knife that she killed him with was in the kitchen sink covered with blood.

I see flames on a fence. But the last cross is mine.
To dwell in a moment constructed of light.

DIXIE J-ELDER
warrants clerk

OFF LIKE A GLOVE

skin slippage
they call it
when the hand
comes off like a glove
after a certain length of time
can't recall how long it takes
but Michael Manning's hands
slipped right off
when the coroner gently tweezed the skin

His mother quit the Air Force
she couldn't focus anymore
divorce, a daughter, a son
& what happened to the baby?
they were living in New York City then.
she told her sister it was adopted
said "it" (OK in Britain, all babies
are called "it" until they've thrived a year
but here, well, it's just weird)

Her sister & mother called the cops after
2 months trying to talk to Michael on the phone
"He's sick in bed" "He's out playing" "He's spending the night
somewhere"

Michael's mother sat in a cell for contempt
she wouldn't talk/hated in silence.
Danny said they sold the boy to some people
from Arizona
$2,000 cash
pretty good money for a skinny little 2-year-old

She wouldn't give their names
or tell how they connected with baby buyers

Was it the cocaine or was cocaine to cure her
of not caring about anything but Danny?
she plucked hairs from his black plastic comb
& tied them into a lock with a piece of elastic

off her black garter
the one she used for a few months
at a massage parlor until the place got shut down
by those damned Boulder cops

They found her voodoo bag under their mattress
after she said she could give them Danny
if they'd just let her out of jail

We sat outside Danny's father's trailer
over on Valmont, near the railroad tracks
& waited for hours
not talking except to hiss
the bastard
the fucking bastard
he FTA'd that night but we got him
                    we got his ass good

I sat with her from 5:00 am 'til 8
no one on duty but us warrants clerks
typewriters silent/detectives all at the scene

she drank water
didn't want to talk/told it all to Bailey at the jail
he cried into the dictaphone it was hard to type up
full of stops, "sorry Dixie"
he believed he'd find a living boy
somewhere in Arizona
but

Danny & she had pulled him out of the heating vent
where they hid him
after Danny beat him to death
for wetting his pants
dug a hole for him near that drainage ditch
where bulldozers parked
ready to tear down the old apartment building

& his hands slipped off like gloves

ANGELO VERGA
former postal worker

BODY IN NEW JERSEY NOT MISSING WOMAN'S

She was decapitated and her hands cut off
By a sharp blade;
There were no other cuts
Or bruises on her body,
And she had been in the lake
For at least seven, and, at most, ten days:
That's what the autopsy said.

Her extrapolated height and weight:
5 feet 9, and one hundred and fifty pounds;
The hair on her torso light brown.
And though the clothes she wore echoed
(Shorts, tee shirt, strapped sandals)
Those of a woman missing
From a neighboring state,

The Lieutenant in Belvedere County
Said she definitely wasn't the same
Woman who'd been missing
In New York for twenty-four days,
Having walked off, it was thought, alone.

We categorically rule that out,
Dennis Cherico explained
These women are not the same.
Birthmarks don't change.
We have two very different, and
Totally unrelated cases here.
Besides, we tried: the head
Won't fit the neck.

WILLIAM HLADKY

detective

WEEPING WALLS

I don't doubt
that your sad story
will make these stark interview-room walls
cry.

I don't doubt
that your father died
when you were ten;
that your mother lost her house
and lives with friends
in a home which has no room
for you;
that you mostly have been homeless
the past five years and
you are not even seventeen years old;
that you're learning disabled
(although you read the Miranda Rights just fine);
that Ms. Rodriguez, a teacher, is the only person
who believes in you
and that you very much want to call her
(but only after you confess);
that your frightened eyes
seek my masculine hug
because I'm the age your father would have been
(and a proper poet would hold you tight,
but I'm not a proper poet);
that your sobbing body shakes with core-deep anguish;
that you speak truth through your tears
when you say you want to die.

Listen to the walls.
They believe you.
Listen to your wails
join the ghostly sobs
of those who came before you here.

The walls tear, however,
not just for your pain,
but because you

relished
towering your 6-foot-2-inch,
two-hundred-forty-pound body
over the woman
you robbed.

Because
you inevitably will twist yourself
to terrorize again
for only while
violating
are you no longer
a victim.

This room moans
because you will
return
to these windowless, white
weeping walls
where I will hug you
(but not tightly)
to get you to confess
to convict your ass.

Fate already has condemned
the rest of you.

MIMI MORIARTY
family life minister

MARRIED TO A COP

Blue lint
    brushed from the sheets
polished shoes
    under the bed
backfire dreams
    a gun in my ribs
as we make love.

He sleeps
    fully clothed
ready for the siren
    someone's emergency
my simple request
    for a calm night's sleep
lost in prestige.

CHARLES RAMMELKAMP

adjunct english professor

ON THE BEAT

When you think of cops,
you don't think of Jamie.
An English major at Urbana,
he joined the Chicago police force,
still under the sinister shroud
of the sixty-eight riots. The reason?
He couldn't get another job.
Who needs another English major?

Once on the South Side mean streets,
his police cruiser stalled in traffic,
the battery dead as his situation seemed.
The meanest-looking dude on the corner
turned a predatory reptilian gaze his way
and peeled himself away from the gang,

He pimped slowly over to a car at the curb,
a scar curling along his jaw
like a coiled snake,
knit black nylon tanktop with a gang logo,
violent tattoos like animal tracks on his arms,
biceps like boulders.
Popped open the trunk.

Nervous, Jamie watched him lean inside,
like a man sticking his body
into the mouth of a whale,
emerged, holding something lethal-looking,
pimped over to Jamie.

"Need a hot shot, man?" he asked,
displaying his jumper cables.

LINDA LANZA

calligrapher, teacher, therapist

MINING FOR EUREKA

"Smell is the mute sense, the one without words."
—Diane Ackerman, *Natural History of the Senses*

A helicopter looms over the front yard.
Two police commiserate in the bedroom,
note the folds, position of sheets, the fist
hole through sheetrock, the uncurtained window.
A forensic specialist surveys the muddied courtyard
behind my house for footprints, traces, tracks.
A uniformed man sits at the chopping block square
of my kitchen table jotting marks in a spiral notebook.
What did he look like? He was tall, I can make
my voice say. About 5'11" I say eyeing the tall
man standing next to him. *Give us a description
so we can look for him.* Tall cop's query
fails to yield the needed clue to identify

the intruder. His smell I try to describe. He smelled
of pheromones singular as fingerprints
the rain has washed from my front room
window he pried loose.   *Turn over*
hissed the voice through shafts of moonlight
casting his shadow on my bed. A mid-range tenor?
a Nevada accent? How much registers in three
notes of a stranger's voice? He was thin, about 150, blond
I respond. The standing officer zooms through the door
into the beam from the whirlybird churning July air.
What else? the jotter wants to know. *Did you know him?*
No I say. Only now his smell I know. The smell.

The cop cocks a brow, scribbles. *What else?*
Socks, no shoes.   *What else?*
I am shivering,
ask for another blanket.   A photographer

snaps shots of my pummeled face, the penknifed sliver
on my left breast. *You're gonna feel it more*
in the morning he tries to soothe me. A white T-shirt,
I say, pulled over his head to mask his face,
came off in the fight. Punched against the wall
I saw stars, the fear in his face. *Amateur*
said a cop. *Probably a neighbor.* I am
not reassured. How long did he practice in his tract
house, jimmying his identical window, secure

he'd gotten his timing down to a rainy weather report?
The question flees. My mind is investigating soul tracks,
imprints made a half hour ago—*probably only ten minutes*
—sniffing inner crevices, a hound scenting underbrush
for fox, searching for smell words to say without equivocation
yes, he did this.   *Come down tomorrow look at books*
see his picture kitchen cop says to a cloud outside the margin
of my hearing. Eyes and ears are not tools for the sense my ravaged
core is honing. My nose is turned inward to the grindstone,
whirling encyclopedically through every dirty shirt
I've laundered, every sweaty man I've bumped against,
every molecule I've ever breathed, labeling and discarding,
sifting and cataloguing, digging in pyrite, mining for eureka.

SARAH CORTEZ
patrol police officer

LINGO

This is how it goes
when you're dating
a cop.

You say, "Will you be home for dinner?"
He says, "Negative."

You say, "Do you like this dress?"
and he says, "It's a good visual."

"Face to face" is a meeting,
not a kiss or a snuggle.
"Fuck you" means hello.
"To dust" is to kill.

On Valentine's when I say
my bra size is 34B,
saying the "B" twice, so
the embarrassing "D" cup
won't be purchased, he
says, "Oh, yeah, 34 BRAVO."
I smile, hoping he'll find
a color lace I don't already have
under my own police uniform.

What isn't said is I love
you. Don't get shot tonight
on shift by a cop-hater. Don't die
before I die, alone
in an alleyway or on a bright street
in widening pools of blood.

STEPHEN DOBYNS
poet & teacher

THE GREAT DOUBTERS OF HISTORY

The woman who kicked out the back window
of the police cruiser sits chain-smoking and
drinking at a table by the dance floor.
Watching from a bar stool, you doubt she
weighs over a hundred pounds. She is gaunt,
bony and resembles a fierce pygmy
warrior. One time she ripped off her clothes
in the parking lot, defied police to touch her.
Another time, she pursued a patrolman
down the street, then kicked him in the balls.
Maybe she's twenty. Here in the bar she
seems jittery, can't hold her liquor, people
tell you, which is probably true but you also
respect someone who knows she has nothing
to lose. You too have nothing to lose but spend
much of your time telling yourself you do.
In fact, it seems the point of society is to
make people think they have something to lose
until a man goes through life as nervously
as if he were carrying a teetery
stack of plates up a dark flight of stairs.

When the woman who kicked out the window
of the cop car dances, she shrugs her shoulders
and stamps her feet very fast as if she
weren't dancing but stamping on a multitude
of grievances. Mostly she dances by herself
because few men will ask her. You nearly
ask her, then change your mind, telling yourself
you are shy; but really you fear that you too
are something she can easily let go,
fear she'll see through your equivocations,
realize you think you have something to lose

and simply guffaw. Why dance with her at all?
Perhaps you think she might instruct you how
to shove aside the trappings of your life,
because in her life nothing's there for keeps,
or so it seems, and you wish you had that
freedom from the things you own, but you don't
so at last you give it up and go home.
It's a clear spring night. In the parking lot,
two cops lean against their cruiser, staring
at the sky and idly waiting for trouble.

Are these the bad guys? Walking to your car,
you think of the fabric of value that surrounds you
as like the night itself, as if you could
poke your finger through it, as if the spots
of light you call stars were the places where
the great doubters of history had jabbed their thumbs.
The younger cop nods hello. You wonder
if they are waiting for the fierce woman
and if you should protect her, remove your
clothes and shout: Take me, take me. But you're not
the one they want in jail. You may have doubts,
but none to break the law for. As you drive home
beside the ocean, the moonpath follows you
on the water like a long finger of light.
Blame me, you say, go ahead, blame me.
Tomorrow you'll buy something you think you'll need,
ditto the next day, ditto the day after that.
Once home, you close and lock yourself inside,
as if you were both guard and prisoner—
prisoner with a question mark in your future
and no days off for your best behavior.

KENNETH DIMAGGIO
son of retired cop

THE PULSE OF THE CITY

As only
others

could tell me

his friends

but also   enemies

like
the old city worker   Stanley
Buckeye

and after
finding out whose son
I was

said you were
a prick

for having
arrested him one night

when he was drunk   even though
he was successfully able to drive his car
in reverse   —the only gear that worked

after he drove his Buick into the Knights
of Columbus Hall

It hurt

not for what he said

if only
you for once were able to say

Instead

it became the dozens

and then the hundreds

of characters

haunting
the Off Track Betting Parlor the
diner the filling station that
still sold gasoline under
the name of Esso

And where most

had agreed

You liked
to talk

and said
things

that made you
the biggest character

driving
the Greek to both swear
and laugh at you

for telling him
not to serve you any
dish that had lamb or

sheep

  because you know what they say
about those mountain village
Greeks

            Telling

the prisoners who had to line
up after a raid

  not to worry

there would be no charge

  for their forthcoming
food   and accommodation

    even they
as everybody else

  had already but with irony
that you ignored   concurred

  you were the pulse of the city

  that finally
had to stop

  when at seventy
one   were given gentle

but still hard for you

retirement that was no longer
deniable

a bitter
muteness

that you now had
for your wife son and daughter

—It was not just
our hands

that you were gracefully
holding

when you first tried
to speak   to both good and

bad alike
succeeding

in letting them no longer
feel like strangers

was just the love
that you could never speak
to us

the love

that you still tried
to give

to the bum   delinquent or
shut-in abandoned and aged
parent

that you always tried to treat

as your family

RODGER L. HILLIARD
military police

SKIN GAMEZZ (PO-PO BLUEZZ)

I be the Po-Po, the Five-O,
but you can call me...Bro'
yo' ass in a fix...
I be the one you oughta know

That's right...I'm that
"Officer...of the Got Dayum Law"
I been on them same streets...
them same corners
and seen the same shit...you saw

Just 'cause I
dress blue
don't mean
I'm any better than you
when I walk down street or into a store
I get that same look...you do

Minus a uniform,
a badge and a gun
I'm that Usual Suspect,
them same fingers
pointed at me...
as if...I was the one

Some expect me to pretend I don't see,
just look away or turn my back,
'cause the skin I'm in...is beautiful black

But I can't pretend I don't see...
just look away or turn my back
Because the skin I'm in...is BEAUTIFUL BLACK!

LC

That's what we call it
In the station
When it isn't a hate crime.
A little gallows humor
To dull the edge.
A term born of frustration.

Black male, 9 years old
Shot dead three blocks from home.

Unmitigated tragedy, yes.
Relegated to obscurity, though.

It could have been otherwise.
He could have been catapulted to fame,
If his killer had been,
Instead of kin,
Someone who looked nothing like him.

But killed by his spitting image—
Another black neighborhood kid—
The victim's name fades.
The outrage subsides.
At present time, no civil suit is pending.

And since his case doesn't constitute a hate crime,
Amongst ourselves
In the stationhouse we say
It wasn't a hate crime.
No, it was a

Love Crime,
Cross referenced under No Big Deal.
The message is clear:
We kill our own.
Everybody understands friendly fire.

PATRICIA CALLAN
mom, playwright, musician

ROAD TEST

She wasn't sixteen.
He made her stop on a hill.
Like a dervish with fifty-five blazing swords,
She flipped cartwheels off curbstones
Knieveled over cars and buses
Ground up the world in her gears.

Blobbed on the road,
a quivering, molded salad of a man;
the trooper (my high school friend)
didn't shake hands.

Flinched, exhaled, *take your mother home.*
Teach her to back up.

SCOTT ODOM
senior deputy sheriff

ABOVE A DARKENED BED

Now I tell of some forgotten woman
Her body, her eyes
The fall of her hair
Her bitten nails
Did not move me

Here is the room she died in—
Twisted sheets
Wine in a puddle on the floor
Scars that traced her skin
The smell of dust
The stillness watching her
Not moving

I was only there a short while
She kept to herself
Gave no indication I was there

I did my work
Then turned away
From the darkened bed
Left others to find her
Somewhere else to sleep

Some will remember
But I will not

I have forgotten her from my mind

BABY J

Moby walks down Twain Avenue
Searching for crack from the passing
Dealers
Carrying his 6 month old daughter in his arms
Like a shield against their violence
C'mon man jus' 10 dollars
Even the sharks don't want to dance with him
His baby shivering in the post dusk chill
Wrapped loosely in a filthy blanket that
Reeks of burnt plastics
His skin is shiny to me
His leprosy showing through in places
Especially his eyes
As I stand him tall in front of my
Ghetto flagship
Red and blue lights bouncing wall to wall
Scaring up the roaches that scuttle endlessly
How the fuck
How the fuck
How the fuck
Can you do that man?
Buy crack with your daughter
In your arms
I imagine some long-lost episode of "Twilight Zone"
Where it's Christmas in Hell and the Zombies shop
With the innocent in tow
Beckoning the shadow demons to
Come close
Come closer
Sell me my need
Don't mind the little one
She's just holdin' my soul for me
Back to the moment I'm just so

Amazed
Amazed
As I hold the fragile infant
In my arms
And see her look at me lost but not afraid
Knowing in her heart that I am here to save her perhaps
But me knowing that sooner than not she will be back
With her crack smoking
Mommy and Daddy
Wandering the world with them
Buying drugs until they die
Or she escapes
Metamorphosis to a butterfly and just
Sails away in the morning breeze
Leaving glass pipes and needle marks
Tattooed on the ground behind her
In a hovel where the miserable clutch themselves and cry
The clay in me becomes just a little
Harder but I let it crack a little so
Some honey can pour out
Just a drop
Just a drop
Enough to sweeten Heaven's tongue in silent prayer
G-d protects drunks and little child-ren so I hope she
Flies I pray she flies I swear she'll fly
As I drop her off at the Clark County Child Protective
Services Building

EDWARD SANDERS
musical activist

PIGASUS

The Yippies decided to run a pig for president
At first Rubin called it Bancroft P. Hogg
but a much better name was found:
                              Pigasus

I went along with it
            hoping it would help stifle
                        a certain use of the name

for I could never join in on the rhythmic chants
of the Panthers at demos:
                "No more brothers in jay-all
                Off th' pi-ig!
                No more brothers in jay-all
                Off th' pi-ig!..."

        just as I thought it was a mistake
        for the Futurists
        to call the Austrian gendarmes
                        "walking pissoirs."

LETTER MY DAD NEVER GAVE ME

Yes, I am a police officer,
but I won't help you become one, too:
if you think my job is fun, son, then you need to know
that every single cop ... becomes an asshole!

Believe me, I didn't start that way.
Back on my graduation day,
I raced to the academy
to join my new, dark blue family:

Like an infantry of wide-eyed, wanna-be soldiers,
we shaved our heads and glared at the sun
like a flock of fuzzy eaglets;
I guess we were all overanxious
to strap on white, round helmets
and charge out of the academy like scrubbing bubbles
sent to sanitize the streets.

But in a matter of weeks,
I absorbed an acidic smell
that splashed me like gasoline...
now I scrub, and I scrub, but I never quite get clean.

For example, consider my discussion with Daryll,
our neighborhood "smack" fiend:
Daryll called at two in the morning to claim some girl
took a tennis racquet to his three-year-old boy
about three weeks before.

   "Damn, Daryll, this better be your dope talking."

Daryll waited with my partner
while I started searching a nearby alley in the rain.
When I came to the sewer drain,
I dropped my light,
so I don't think anyone saw me
drop in the dirt, dig in the drain
    and touch

the torn, rotten flesh
of a beautiful, broken, black baby boy
who never expected an asshole cop
would be the last one on earth
to cradle him close and kiss his cheek.

    "So...you still want my job, son?"

Then try to keep your hands from shaking
as you try to console a sobbing, single mother
who just found vaginal tears
on her two-year-old daughter.

    "How well can you lie?"

Tell mom the baby will be just fine,
tell her to believe in justice,
or tell her the truth
about what she's done:

In her hurry to clean the baby's blood
from her brother's salty, warm, infected come
she just washed away the evidence,
now no one will do a day for this crime.
No matter what you say this time, son,
you're gonna feel like you just renounced your soul.
So go home.

Take a bath and bask in the beautiful fragrance of naïveté,
understanding
there's an awful lot of death in life no one should see,
and son, I need you to leave that world to me...
not because I'm selfish but because I believe
that I've become the asshole
I never wanted you to be.

GIL FAGIANI

social work administrator

FIRST DAY IN EL BARRIO

We were six students
three men and three women
on summer break
living in El Barrio
and volunteering to work
with a local antipoverty agency
It was our first day in the neighborhood
and a police officer
with an Italian nametag
came to our door
and warned us to watch our step
He recalled that
when he began his beat in the Barrio
he was young and idealistic
like us and wanted to help
the poor and downtrodden
But in no time he learned
that except for a tiny group of residents
too scared to say a word
the majority of people
were backstabbers, sneaks
junkies, welfare bums,
dope addicts and cutthroats
We argued with him
brought up the twin evils
of racism and poverty
He laughed
said we had too many
books on the brain
while his knowledge came from the streets
Before leaving he gave his card
and a wink
to the three women

encouraging them to call him
After the cop had gone
we sat around cursing him
for his cynicism
and hateful attitude
when we heard
the banging of steps
up high
and somebody shouting:
"¡*Me gusta!*
¡*Me gusta!*
¡*Me gusta!*"
"Where is the noise coming from?"
"Somebody is running down from the roof"
The knocking grew louder
and the voice more insistent
"¡*Me gusta!*
¡*Me gusta!*
¡*Me gusta!*"
"What does *me gusta* mean?"
"It means *I like it*"
"Let's go out on the stairway"
We crowded on the filthy tile landing
just as a young man
charged past us
with curly black hair
olive skin
handsome as Sal Mineo
but with eyes popping out
and a belt dangling from his arm
"¡*Me gusta!*
¡*Me gusta!*
¡*Me gusta!*"
he chanted
as he flew down the steps
and out the building

C.L. KNIGHT
ex-wife of ex-cop

THE WALL

Helena hits the wall.
She is immediately silent, while an explosion of metal
and steam surrounds her mother. The seat is empty
where Helena slept when the car began
its slow-motion skid, turning, spinning,
hydroplaning into the warehouse wall.
Helena, Helena where are you?

The distant wail of sirens spills into my dreams.

You pull a twisted woman from the wreckage.
She is screaming louder now, *Helena, Helena ...*
You find her baby—a pale bundle of yellow
strangely flat on the asphalt.

At 2 a.m.
the paperwork is done,
the mother sedated,
the baby at the morgue.

While I sleep, fingers curled in the edge of a blanket,

you shed your uniform shirt
and gunbelt, stash them in the trunk
and head for the Boots and Saddle Bar;
to be washed in thick blue smoke
and the harp-sad sound of a juke box.

Other men in white T-shirts, shiny black lace-ups
and almost-black blue pants straddle barstools or
lean into the wall and drink their beer from cloudy glasses.
You tell the joke about the lawyer and the alligator.
Everyone laughs and no one

mentions babies,
even their own at home asleep,
where they will go when last call echoes
through the neon funk and they must leave.

In the parking lot, the beat of rain has flatlined
and left a glistening silence between the cars.

RICK FOURNIER

retired schoolteacher

PLAYING GUNS IN WEST DULUTH

Even when I saw   in what seemed
Like slow motion   the disgusted policeman
Draw and aim   his .38 caliber revolver
Smith and Wesson   Police Special
At ten years old   I knew guns
Knew Colt   knew Smith and Wesson
Knew Iver Johnson   Hi Standard

I couldn't believe   he would really shoot
Down into the head   of Donnie's dog
A white terrier   I had shot so often
With my cap pistol   or my cork-popping rifle
When he was a bear   or a lion or tiger
Who now thrashed about   on the soft turf
Alongside the street   his back broken

We kids watched   and held our breath
We knew this dog   but not this officer
Nor the driver   of the killer car
Who stood helpless by   trying to explain

Donnie and family   were not there
To witness   this excitement
This streetside drama   marked by the roar
Of a real pistol   a .38 caliber revolver
Held by a grim-faced cop   so steady
I could see worn spots   on the bluing
Then he fired   and Donnie's dog went limp
After being slammed   against the ground
A small hole   behind his ear
His blood   soaking the ground beneath

We all exhaled together   thinking the same
Terrible thought: who was going to tell Donnie?

PASQUALE BOTTIGLIERI
schoolteacher

WALKING WITH WILD HORSES

Silence
is a fearful thing
on the street.

Light
streams down
in slanted
shafts
through fetid
smoke filled
air.

There are no
sounds
save
the scurry
of little claws
on discarded cardboard.

Cobblestones
ahead
wet with dew
lay scattered

a jigsaw puzzle
disturbed
by curious children
a piece gone here
two awry there.

Now
a pothole
packed with garbage

and someone's
filthy
underwear
slips between
barely rolling
tires.

The "El"
is ahead
just ahead
across the cluttered street

rising up
out of the weeds
like a sad old man
in graffiti stained clothes.

Boxes, crates
piled, strewn
broken glass glinting.

Here

it smells
like burning
Brillo pads.

Then comes
a faint whimper
so slight
the mildest breeze
would smother it.

Now
silence.

Another cry
muffled
this time
sharper
urgent.

Again
silence.

Now
a gasping moan

dead ahead.

From
behind the crates
a movement.

Time becomes
liquid
pouring out
slowly
thickly
second by second
a blur
of

engine sounds
crackling radio
flashing lights
pitched voices
and
labored breathing.

Sweat
suddenly
comes in rivulets
running
down the barrel
of a pistol
held outstretched
with both hands.

The man
face down
on the ground
blinks
as droplets
of sweat
splash
on the back
of his head.

Illuminated
scant feet away
brown hair askew
eyes half open
mouth agape
she lies
finished with life
a piece of dirty rope
still tight
around
her neck.

Husband

Father of three
Officer of the Law
he
breathes slowly
through clenched teeth.

The wild horses
have come and gone.

In this land

it is certain

that
they will come
again.

CULTURE

It's a cultural thing
to say *give me* a lo mein,
give me a soda.

It's a cultural thing
to swing around the corner
in your livery cab,
disregarding the pedestrians'
right-of-way.

It's a cultural thing
to hawk up a wad of phlegm
in close proximity to a person
then spit it on the sidewalk
not in the gutter.

It's a cultural thing
to piss next to a dumpster
on my street, in daylight,
then pass the culture on
to your three-year-old
by getting him to piss there too.

It's a cultural thing
to stand on the station platform
in front of a subway-car door,
then push into the wall
of people trying to exit.

It's a cultural thing
to cross someone's path
without as much as looking at him.

It's a cultural thing,
after taking the cabby's money,
to shoot him twice in the head
so there'll be no one to report the crime.

It's a cultural thing
to toss a bucket of plaster
off the roof of a six-story building
onto a police officer's head
because he's writing tickets
on double- and triple-parked cars.

It's a cultural thing
for our mayor to have had the city pay
for the funeral of the "victim"
of a policeman's bullet—before a
proper investigation, which revealed
the "victim" as having been
an established drug dealer
in possession of a gun.

It's a cultural thing
to pitch a Molotov cocktail
into a fire engine rushing
into your street, brought there with
a false alarm.

It's a cultural thing
to bash in a man's head
because he happened to be where
it was the cultural thing for a jury
to acquit policemen
who had done their cultural thing by
kicking-in the ribs of a man in the
prone position, who had been doing
his cultural thing of getting stoned
out of his mind and acting-out.

It's a cultural thing,
your calling me a racist
because I didn't think your poem
about culture
was good enough for my magazine
—or because I, a registered democrat
this time voted for the white republican
federal prosecutor
in our mayoral election.

SOPHIE HUGHES
retired art teacher

FALLING BODY

A vast updraft of air
a weighty WHOOSH
and then the thud—
final, hard.
I'd heard that sound before
and moved with dread
to my window, in the
court below a body:
fully clothed, white-haired,
legs splayed, arms crossed
hugging his shoulders
the way one does
on lying down to sleep.
I notified the doorman.
Before long a bevy of cops
surrounded the corpse,
examining for any sign
of life. Detectives turned
the head face-up to photograph.
Two young police stepped back,
weakly joked, while one
compared the real to a TV film
he'd seen that "did it better."
All dispersed except
the eldest cop who
stood guard alone.
He studied long that gentle
expression of utmost peace.
Slowly he raised his head
to the sky above,
and heaved a heavy sigh.

DAVID G. EPSTEIN
law enforcement administrator

UNTITLED #3

i once thought that i
owned a bunch of streets
that were in a city with
palm trees and
live oaks with
spanish moss hanging
from the branches
and cockroaches who
covered the sidewalks after
the sun let the dark out
into the night
rushing around eating
garbage
before the rains washed it away and
into the river
that ran by the city and
into the sea
i've often wondered
what does cockroach shit
look like?
i mean it must really be
gross
and i've often wondered
if my deed to those streets
meant as much to the people
sleeping on sweat wet sheets
behind open windows into which
no wind ever blew
the paper bag factory smelling air
as it did to those cockroaches.
and on other streets in
the city with
palm trees and live oaks

where slept the people
in homes of the just
where windows never had to be opened
and the sheets were only wet with sweat
two or three times a week
at most
whose justness was rewarded
by a god who bestowed
riches as a reward for
justness
and whose cockroaches were dealt with by
terminex and
people like me
who owned the streets.

ANN CEFOLA
creative strategist

THE TOWN WHERE HE LIVED

I ain't never seen the street this quiet, one woman says to another,
whose orange hair blows in the breeze as they cross the empty Post Road.

Thin blue and black ribbons flutter on telephone poles. Carnations,
red and pink, weight wire easels outside the police station, the deli.

Outside Immaculate Conception, the hum, the vibrato of hundreds
     of motorcycles,
chrome and white roaring in place, officers chatting, focused elsewhere.

The journalists with cameras, notepads, microphones. Moved back
     home for a safer job.
Often let crossing-guards warm up in his car. *Go on,* he'd insist. *I'll take over.*

The long blue line, uniformed policemen four deep, all the way down
     Winter Hill Road.
The shouts of the commander, *company this, company that, be back at 10:45 a.m.*

Richard Saachi, Jr. Due back at Riker's. No one getting in his way:
     neither his grandmother,
nor his dog. Not even that first cop who pulled up, easy, like a carnival
     target.

The cocktail party atmosphere outside the church. The droning of
     dignitaries inside.
The priest: *We don't know what awaits on the other side. But where
     God is, there is love.*

Coming out of the drugstore, a man looks up. Helicopters. My car radio:
It has been confirmed. That officer in Eastchester has died. My throat
    thick and hot.
The town supervisor: *They will say our town is where Michael Frey was killed.*
No! We must say it is where he lived.
The coffin, borne slowly out of the church. The widow, held up on each
    side, samples air
like foul food. Giuliani. Bratton. Taps, the brass sound, stunning
    each officer.

Frey's partner crawling to the ground. Before shooting himself to
    heaven or hell,
Saachi writing on the wall *I'm sorry. I just want to be with Jesus.*

Three helicopters which rise from behind the church like bubbles
    floating through water,
and still the quiet, the long blue line, the church bell now, the spring
    wind lifting.

ANGELO VERGA
former postal worker

EX-COP SLAIN IN MOTEL

The next day
a 30-dollar room
his drained and naked face
stains a multicolored rug.

They took his car and credit cards
and bought leather vests and gold chains
on Christopher Street, an exuberant promenade.

The boys, 16 and 18,
camouflage jackets, mohawk haircuts
held sway also in Tompkins Square Park,
hoodwinking numerous overweight johns.

Those who breed, Darwin taught us,
pass their genes on.

An ex-detective and former tough guy named Dave
out of step, out of shape
head busted, bashed in
by sharp-edged porcelain bathroom tile,
throat cut, veins slashed—at length
his corpse claimed by straight-laced, apostolic cousins
who reside on Long Island.

No slow adaptive process,
crimes evolve
        (like love itself,
or perhaps justice)
by choices made
        to rise up
        or fall down.

AHIMSA TIMOTEO BODHRÁN

artist, activist, academic

NYPD BLUES

(or the youngest homicide my father can remember)

newborn
baby
girl

one n a half
minutes
old

raped by her
father
blood

all over the walls
hair-flesh
pieces of

meat
chunk-like
everywhere

he
there
at the scene of the crime

wondering not why
he is beyond why
but rather how

u have
the chalk
but where do u draw

the

line

THOMAS J. OBRZUT
social worker

RETIRING

I remember
Years before
Suit pressed
Laid out
That smell of clean
And the gun
Oiled
Shiny, not knowing what was coming.

Mary smiling
Made eggs and bacon
Pots of steaming coffee
On our days off
Her from the kids in PS 27
Me from walking down Delancey
My feet still hurting
But thinking about Epsom salts
And watching college ball on the tube.

Later, after Patrick was born
We moved out of Hell's Kitchen
To Long Island for back yards, cars, patio grills
PJ growing up
Should've known from that red hair
There was going to be trouble
Nothing major though
He was wild
Reminded me of me
Anyway he's a cop now too
Has a kid
Patrick III.

Times weren't always good though
Not everyone in the neighborhood
Felt the same as Mr. Schwartz
Who gave me knishes and sometimes
       Hot corned beef
Refused to take money
Not everyone felt that way
Especially in the bad days
When you could buy heroin in every Laundromat
I remember once
Kid's name was Punky
Everyone called him that
He was crazy
I already busted him three or four times
First when he was twelve
Later he got bigger
And meaner too
He was running some kind of business
Right there on Third Street
When I told him it was time
That he was being called out
He took it seriously
I never even pulled my gun
Got three shots to the chest
Good thing for me
Kid couldn't shoot straight
I got a year on disability
He's still in jail

Funny thing is out of all those years
It's something Punky said
Sticks with me to this day
I was laying on the ground
Couldn't believe what happened
Punky didn't even run
I looked up at him
"Why'd you do that?" I asked
Punky just shook his head
"I don't know," he said,
"Never shot a cop before."

SARAH CORTEZ
patrol police officer

RIDE-ALONG

Another cop tells me
about the female
doing the Ride-along
when Sobo got killed.

Him lying there bleeding
bad; her not knowing
to push the radio button
down when you talk.

That kid didn't shoot
her even though he
knew she saw
the whole thing.

He stared at her
hard through the
windshield, holding
his gun, deciding.

She didn't even know
the name of the street
or the hundred block
to tell Dispatch.

So, once the kid ran
she crawled out
the shop to Sobo, turned
him over, held his hand, recited

the Our Father with him
while he died. This
other cop says
he heard she moved

out of Houston. Went
up East. Came back
to testify against the kid.
Had a nervous breakdown.

My Ride-alongs—I
show them the radio
button. Me—I
want an ambulance.

TOM PADILLA

nephew & grandson of nyc policemen

ON HIS LAST TOUR

—for George Walsh

The cop on desk-duty took the call—"an EDP with a knife, Throgs
    Neck Bridge, request for backup." The perp groped
a toll booth clerk, who later said he'd looked fierce
as last week's blizzard, the city low on salt.
This cop, time-hardened, stared down the young Sarge, eye to eye.
I'll take it, he said. *Finish your orange*

juice. Sarge nodded Yeah. A few minutes later, orange
lights pinwheeling on the roof-rack, he passed a jackknifed
tractor-trailer, another victim of the ice.
News choppers, TV vans with telescoping
antennae—even newshound cabbies—sped to the assault.
First things first, however; fear's

the enemy. *This mutt's going down*, the cop thought, *pierced
nose, and all.* In the rearview mirror, a Range
Rover skidded in slush. In the windshield, ready to pour salt
on an open wound, was the weirdo wielding a bowie knife.
And on the police cruiser's back seat, the Y-shaped grappling
device—built to handle these kinds of jobs with minimal force—
   and a can of pepper spray.

An eye for an eye.
About to do fierce
battle, the cop thought, *If this mutt had groped
one of my daughters*…Slamming on the brakes, the orange-
and-blue EMS truck, responding to the same call—"Emotionally
   Disturbed Person with knife"—
sent an arc of rock salt

high into the air. Jumping out, two young medics, in green—
not at all like the cop and his old partner, an ex-Navy salt.
The cop eyeballed the scene: the knife,
the news crews—and with a fierce
crack of his old nightstick to the wrist, he sent
  the glinting weapon into the orange-
tinted waves below. The perp now groped

the asphalt, but all his grope
was gone. Wrist broken in three places, saline
was administered by syringe.
While the police, EMS, cabbies, and news people did not always
see eye to eye, the cop of thirty-five years
thanked them all for their part. This cop was getting out
without getting sliced.

PERPETRATORS

DAVID MILLS

cave canem writer

ALL 4-1

"There is no hunting like the hunting of man and those
who have hunted armed men long enough like it
and never really care for anything else hereafter."
———Ernest Hemingway

I

Their clothes are plain
And their cars unmarked. They own
The night and rent out stars to whichever
Sky they can frisk, to whichever sky
Puts in the highest bid. This one is
Fickle and bruised, it's the moon
Sucked through a straw like vanilla milk.
This sky is smeared over Wheeler
Avenue in the Bronx. This evening
This slim Guinean kid is going to pay
The North Star's electric bill.
He is sliced pineapples and iron; succulent
Diamonds and beans. A peddler
Of answers to winter's bitter questions.
And when he counts crisp singles
His words skip like a needle
On a scratched LP.
He also hawks Hip-hop. He could
Never understand the 187 on an undercover
Cop. The way young tongues pop
Shit and then argue with the air
For turning sour and brown.
He couldn't understand how a place
Bubbling over with skyscrapers
Could be called the Village. It is nothing
Like the thatched huts and plump dust of Kindia.
But these clean-cut, trigger-happy, concrete
Cowboys are looking for someone. Illegal

Gun possession, then they're on the hunt for a rapist,
Then a serial rapist, then a serial rapist murderer
Or an unidentified caller reported a man
In a hallway acting human,
Which fit the victim's description.
They asked him not to
Move as he jiggled an object
In the vestibule. His wallet,
Which might have resembled a gun,
Or his pager, that might have resembled a pistol;
Or he was breathing steel so
The bones beneath their hands
Became as supple as smoke
As they rat a tat tat, rat a tat tat,
Rat a tat tat, rat a tat tat,
Purump-pump-pump-pump
Pump-pump-pump-pump
Pump-pump-pump-pump
41 shooting stars all for one slim kid
Who they send back to his mother-
Land in morsels. Dead. His top lip
Twitches like a lost sea looking
For sand, looking for an answer
To this. His heart broke
Through bone, a concrete balloon,
That drifts and withers inches
Above this tough love.

II

They even frisked the bag
Of vanilla sticks in his bedroom
And wanted to know if he
Had enemies not telling us
That their hands were white hot
With the death of my cousin.
They hoped his record
Was scratched; they didn't know

Each of his fingers was a prayer
His thumb, dawn; his index, noon; the tips
Of his middle and ring finger, before
And after sunset; and his pinky, midnight;
They didn't know during Ramadan
The sun is a hungry belly
That rises and sets between a camel's humps.
They didn't know that this vestibule was his minaret
And that as he fell his shadow snapped
And hobbled around this filthy sky
Seven times. He made his pilgrimage
Kissing the concrete as if
It were the Kaaba's holy stone.
Lean your ear against the smoldering volcanoes
Dotting his body, listen to the riddles bullets
Tell: Allahu Akbar! They claim to own the night
Let's repossess it. Here and now
Is what we hate.

ANDREW KAUFMAN
english professor

A PANTOUM FOR SERGEANT KOON

*Sergeant Stacey Koon was the senior officer involved in the videotaped beating of
Los Angeles motorist Rodney King. Koon was eventually convicted and sentenced to
a prison term for violating King's civil rights.*

Reaching down as though for a weapon,
the suspect appeared under the influence of crack cocaine.
When eight officers could not place him under restraint,
the sergeant tried to subdue him with the Taser gun.

Since he appeared under the influence of crack cocaine,
struggling to the point of convulsions,
my client had no choice but to use the Taser gun.
When this had no effect the police became alarmed.

Struggling to the point of convulsions,
the suspect forced the officers to use their batons.
When this had no effect it heightened their alarm.
Mr. King then went into the "Folsom roll," to seize a gun,

forcing the officers, once more, to use their batons.
The sergeant must protect his men.
Poised, in the "Folsom roll," to seize a gun,
by continuing to struggle, the suspect controlled the action.

The sergeant, remember, has to protect his men.
When the suspect resumed struggling he was stomped on.
Keep in mind that the suspect controlled the action.
Once he stopped struggling the incident came to an end.

When he resumed the struggle he was stomped on.
The police adhered to Departmental guidelines;
once he stopped struggling, the incident came to an end.
Again: he's on his back, right there—leg cocked, to attack them.

The police adhered, at all times, to Departmental guidelines.
Eight officers could not place him under restraint.
Here—look once more—he cocks his legs to attack them
while reaching down, as though for a weapon.

WANDA COLEMAN

cultural activist

SOUTH CENTRAL CHEAP THRILLS

you have not lived
until two uniforms knock on your door
at sunrise with a warrant for your arrest
because you did not pay
that poot-butt parking ticket
because what little money you earn
goes first to the landlord,
second to feed your kids the sugar, salt and starch
they need to keep breathing

you have not lived
until you've outrun a prowl car in midmorning
casing your headgear
until you make a U-turn
against traffic, then a right onto a residential street
turn into the driveway of someone's home
duck down in the seat praying they've passed you
monitoring that rearview to make certain
the cops are gone—in this reality
imitating the movies

you have not lived
until you're arrested in front of neighbors
a half block from home
for having a broken taillight
then having them search your car and purse
for contraband (when you don't even smoke)
then taking your children into custody
while you're pushed head first into the backseat
of the patrol car
on suspicion of harboring radical thoughts

you have not lived until
you've seen fear and confusion
in your children's eyes, knowing mommy
has done something
wrong or else these nice policemen
would not be arresting her

you've missed the all-time thriller diller
if you've never seen flashes of anger
and contempt
wash away all innocence
in a wall of tears

you are not blessed until you've
lost a major opportunity
because officers have spotted you and
are frisking you
because you're dressed in clothes
that identify you (in their minds) as trouble
as domineering as a thugster
you don't know from ice ice, baby
until they force you against the hood
and handcuff you in front of the executives
who were about to hire you for the job
that would have liberated you from poverty

you have not lived until you've felt the
fingers and hands
of a hard and handsome officer
probe your hair and crotch
for marijuana or bullets, telling you
what kind of bitch
he thinks you are and what
he would love to do to you
were you his

(when your father
goes down for grand larceny,
when your brother the boy scout
is rousted and taken to juvenile hall,
when your lover
is made to drop drawers in front of homies,
when your partner
is pistol-whipped for being flippant,
when every blood in your neighborhood
is guilty of kidnapping and rape, well—
then, maybe)

womanhood will never be the same
after you've felt the barrel of a gun
to your head, watching the sweaty masculine
hand that holds it
tremor and jiggle while you wonder
about the odds in favor
of its discharging a round
sending you to the state crematorium
and your children to an orphanage

you have not lived
until you've been ushered into the world
of luckless women, the hardcore
and the soft
who people the digs for desperate dames
until you've laid there in the dark
combing the insides of your eyeballs
wondering who you can hit up for the money
it's gonna take
dreaming while awake

you have not lived
until you've been stopped and questioned

WILLIAM HLADKY

detective

THE INTERROGATION

Come here.
I want to show you something.
Not too close.
I don't want you to fall.
What do you see?
It's the abyss.
Pretty damn deep, huh?
Scary looking.
Dark. No light down there.
Do you want to be thrown in?
Of course not.
You'll never get out.
I want to help you.
You're not like most people I deal with.
Most people I deal with are hard core.
You deserve a break.
You just got caught up in something.
I know people who can help you.
I can't make any promises,
but I can talk to them.
I've been working with them for years.
They respect my work.
They respect my opinion.
Of course, I can't make any promises.
But you have to give me something to work with
so I can say you're worth helping.
They don't want you down there
anymore than you want to be down there.
It's crowded enough with people who refused to help themselves.
Give me something.
Now is the time to tell me your side of the story.
Go on.
Okay.

Okay.

By the way, how many times did you say you did it?

Don't hold back now.

You already have taken that first step to help yourself.

That's good.

Let me write this down.

Would you mind if we go over your story again with a tape recorder?

You would protect yourself putting it on tape.

I won't be able to change anything when I write my report.

Don't you feel better?

You say you feel like you are falling.

You're just light-headed from our talk.

QURAYSH ALI LANSANA
father, professor, editor

OUR SONS

for the seven- and eight-year-old boys wrongly accused
in the murder of eleven-year-old Ryan Harris

the difference between
the truth and a lie

separates a one-inch skull
fracture and a rock
chucked by a seven-year-old.

blue beads grip
his braids, jerking
as he nods in response.

if he grows up
he hopes to join
chicago's finest gang.

they drive fast cars,
carry big guns,
always live on tv.

just a few more questions, ma'am.

the wooden bench
no more comfortable
than it has ever been.

in chicago, justice is
a room with no windows.

her boy, seven, is hungry,
confused. she can feel it
from the muffled hallway.

door cracked. dark
as frantic shadows.
daddy is not allowed

to enter the station.
guards hold back
fire. the englewood moon

a pale, knowing bulb.

the boys, low-rent refugees
from third world corners,
bend, then break: confess

over happy meals. they will be
forgotten like quiet bicycles.

HANK KALET
newspaper editor & columnist

PICTURE OF A COP'S WIFE

The purple under her eye
is a sure sign
of danger
    a signal that
the violence of his job has
spilled from his shift and is
leaving its mark on her face.

KEN MCMANUS

civil servant

NIGGER REFLEX

I

As the police line-up of stars ambles in
A cease-and-desist moment takes place as he
Protests his belonging here:
"I didn't.../ I wasn't even.../ I'm not..."
Bam.
One simple look from the angled eye of a lantern-jawed cop
Stops him.
His face goes slack, his arms fall to his sides, his muscles rid themselves
     of bone,
His suit jacket drapes close to his shoulders, he
Empties his self of false resistance just as
His body shirks the burden of carrying innocence
He faces forward,
Turns left, Turns right
And shows nothing
As the rage flaring in his chest is reduced to a temporary cold ember
In the pit of his stomach.

II

"Well, she didn't mark you this time, boy;
Now just you stay out of trouble,"
the cop says, laughing, garlicky breath flicking at his nostrils
His senses begin to power up:
A wetness under his arms,
Tingling sensations in his scalp, shortened respiration
He gathers his things in his numbed hands,
Barks the heel of another carnival-goer in front of him
And then the night air assaults his senses
As he makes his way on stiff legs
Down the boulevard.

TYEHIMBA JESS
musician, activist, artist

JOHN BURGE, RETIRED

i am justice,
my wooden river of nightstick
slamming bruise into back,
my stiffened blur of motion
suspended over dusky skin.

in this room we all played our roles,
telephone book and radiator ready
to silent witness, water bucket
brimming for prisoner's breath,
green garbage bag a folded vigil
for another nigger-lipped gasp.

and always, always, my hands.

this is not about confession.
this is about justice,
fiery cure we all swallow
to make things right.
every painted hide i cuffed
added a tooth to this city's
prison capped grin,
every fisted inch of flesh
pushed the stock market higher,
let the public know safety
is dressed in blue and won't
take no for an answer.

they still need me here.
even the ones who bitch and moan
would rather hear of my sweated uppercut

and stranglehold ballet wielding fear's wisdom
in this interrogation room
than to see a hooded spook
in their garage one night.

the public put me here, gospel of pain
soldered into my mind, bat in hand
and badge glowing fierce
in the love i have for my job.

my first police action was Da Nang,
our beating room a tent in the field
where we learned the genius of steel clamped
to scrotum and wired to a field telephone's
electric charge, how cranking the handle like you're calling home
is enough to roast a man's balls.

so here, when i would twist that
jack-in-the-box handle and watch
a boy's buck-danced eyes explode
with the truth i'd tell 'em to sign for
on the dotted line—it was just like old times:
when we painted 'Nam countryside
a color of bomb we now only dream
of matching, cell by cell, in the gun-
metal grey of prison bars.

but war is so political these days,
and like old times,
a few pansies get in the way
of my flesh and blood machine,
throw up a few picket signs,
think they've severed the snake's head
when they push me out of a job.
fuck it.

i still got my pension, my houseboat,

my memories and legacy of all
my synchronized, soldiered men.

they can't take that away.

i was a regular fuckin school of the americas.
and we are just like them jews
cause baby, we never forget.

like today.
today i took a trip into this zoo
called chicago, came to this old station
where my commander's number is retired,
and on my way to this cinderblocked room,
the old ones still knew me.

didn't say a word.
paused.
gave salute.

MICHAEL CASEY
teacher

ROES AND THE NIGHTSTICK

Trooper Rolla of Troop I
Missouri State Highway Patrol
has brought in an AWOL
and while subject AWOL is in the cage
the Trooper shows off his mace
to us his colleagues of a different jurisdiction
says he's never used it but once
and knows it works
but he'd much rather have his club
which impresses people visually first
and then more particular if they get hit
on the haid with it
and Trooper jokes
asks Roes if he'd like to swap
Trooper's mace for Roes' club
and Roes gets all indignant
Roes has worked hard on his club
took considerable trouble
to scrounge a drill and soldering iron
to insert lead solder into the tip
Roes will talk about the attempted swap weeks later
how that breeder wanted his club
but Roes has been to the third grade
and knows a trick
Roes says he was born at night
but not last night

NAT READ
LAPD

STREET JUSTICE

O'Malligan Hopp was the neighborhood bully;
O'Malligan Hopp was the neighborhood thug.
He brought down the worth of the neighborhood houses
By simply parading his miscreant mug.

Again and again we were called to his address.
Again and again he would spit in our face.
We lectured, we warned him, we booked him and booked him,
But always the system made light of his case.

"Enough is enough!" said one cop to another.
"Enough is enough! We will settle this feud!"
We gassed him to hamper his breath and his vision
Then working together we roughed up the dude.

Adjusting our halos, we framed our report:
"Right out of the blue Mr. Hopp charged our face.
We fended him off for as long as we could, but
To finally subdue him we had to use mace."

The court saw it our way, the court locked him up.
The court disbelieved him, the court ruled for us.
The neighborhood's calm now without Hopp's abuse,
He came back behumbled, avoiding all fuss.

So street justice worked when the system betrayed us.
So street justice worked through a dosage of might.
The end in this case upheld all of our methods.
But honestly, friend, it still wasn't right.

AN OPERATION

A couple of policemen dressed
        In plain-clothes best,
Like auto dealers pushing forty,
        Straight and yet sporty,
Sat, one on show and one confined
        To a room behind
The storefront rented in pretence
        It was a fence
—Fly-blown, and on a corner-lot
        Realtors forgot:
So to draw out a neighborhood's
        Just-stolen goods,
And sweep up drifts of petty thieves
        As thick as leaves.

They sent out word and waited while
        The slow shy file
First dribbled in then wouldn't stop.
        The hidden cop
Taped the transactions of the crooks
        Who filled the books
The other kept, practical, blunt,
        Front of a front.

No doubt encouraging some few
        To come into
A school of thieves, a new career,
        Who had stayed clear,
Such cops would view themselves as al-
        legorical,
Unaltered by what they had done
        So long as one,
At a desk somewhere, in the cells,

Or somewhere else
(In heaven?), could still tell a sting
From the real thing,
And keep their interesting position
Above suspicion.

They had grown up with paradox
And other shocks,
Spaced out with regulation jokes,
Coffee, and smokes,
In traps that looked like other traps.
But they got maps.
They'd both been in Vietnam, and knew
That often you
Have to destroy to liberate.

And if you wait,
Tilting your chair almost at spill,
A sort of thrill
Steals upward to the skin maybe,
Til you are free
To stretch within an innocence
Born from constraints.
Like spies who fornicate to steal,
You like the feel,
And sweat into the extended play,
While day by day
Behind plate-glass flies buzz, get old,
And cups grow cold.

TIFF HOLLAND
dispatcher, copwife

WORKING NARCOTICS

First, you get a snitch,
a C.I., confidential informant,
someone you've already busted.
Buy-bust probably.
First you buy, talking shit:
   thanks man, I really need a hit,
then badge-flash,
smile twisting into leer, bust.
   Yeah, need to bust your sorry ass,
handcuffs, and Miranda, and
the Bad News talk:
   We got you;
   we know you been slinging this shit but
   it's your lucky day.
   You can work your way out of prison,
   work for us
and because prison is too far away
from the next high
the snitch agrees.

You wire the C.I. up
using a fake pack of smokes
with a hidden mike, or
a converted beeper,
something the dealer's hands won't find,
patting the snitch down at the door.
This way the undercover cop
you send in with him
goes in clean.
Sometimes the cop is questioned,
white, after all, after dark in McElrith,
but cops lie well:

I ain't no fucking cop
each one learns to say with sincerity
and a look of true disgust.

After a few buys, there's a raid,
swat teams, and shouting,
a search of the house,
everything dumped:
everything from the underwear drawers,
to the cornflakes box
because dopers hide it any place,
inside the toilet, or the kid's lunch box,
wrapped in plastic bags in the clothes hamper,
or the bottom of a dog food bag.
The money is hidden, too,
thousands filed in shoeboxes,
under loose boards in a closet, or
a hole dug out back in the toolshed.

Soon the snitch has turned everyone he knows,
all his friends,
relatives, too.
If he's done enough, you let him go,
let him off the hook,
sometimes with a little cash
to get away
from everyone he has betrayed.
A grand maybe,
and a Greyhound ticket
for a good snitch
with a price on his head, but
it doesn't matter what's typed on that ticket.

They all come back.
Months later you read about
Gumby or Pinky or Gator
in the local paper,

beaten to death out in the projects,
maybe by someone he's turned
but just as likely by a dealer he's stiffed,
the last high
just beginning to fade
as the Maglite comes down on his head,
or the ball bat
or the tire iron.
No one listening now,
from inside the van,
no one saying,
   this is your lucky day.

DENISE DUHAMEL
creative writing professor

WHAT HAPPENED THIS WEEK
(May 1, 1992)

David didn't come to school Tuesday,
the day his essay was due.
Instead the police showed up—
a Dragnet team—asking if anyone
had seen him since Friday.
The class huddled at the implications
of the words: missing person.
David, eighteen, too old for milk cartons,
but just ripe for the morgue
and a numbered tag around his bare toe.
Just ripe for a knife, a bullet,
a bat. He was gentle, small enough to be raped
then stored in a car trunk
if there was time, or left on a subway platform
with his empty wallet by his head.
When I called his mother the next day
the phone didn't ring a full ring before she picked it up.
Not having slept, she couldn't remember her address
when I said David's English class
wanted to send her a card.
She said David was the first of his family
to go to college. I told her he wrote
beautiful essays, then I said, "I mean, he *writes*
beautiful essays," trying to keep him alive
by using present tense. When he showed up
to class on Thursday, we all thought we were seeing
his ghost. Blue bruises tinted his black forehead,
like a halo collapsing inward.
He said he'd been arrested in East New York,
and we all clapped because he was still alive.
He told the story—stopped as a passenger
in a stolen car, which, of course, turned out

not to be stolen after all.
"Run, so I can shoot you, nigger,"
a policeman said to David
who shook and whirled inside
like a blender. He had to concentrate
on his feet, keeping them steady
so there'd be no mistake about any sudden movements.
He was tossed in a cell, questioned
about the two hundred dollars in his front pocket
since he was on his way to buy his girlfriend
a ring for her birthday. The white cops
made fun of his musk oil, stepped on his sunglasses
though, he was assured later, this was by mistake.
Though everyone in America is still entitled
to that clichéd one call, this particular jail
in East New York didn't have a pay phone
that worked. David cried into his cot,
and the guard called him a mama's boy,
hitting him, heel of his palm to David's head.
No phone, they laughed the first 48 hours,
and the tri-state Dragnet team took two more days
after that to find him, even though
he was in one of their own jails.
David told us his story Thursday morning,
and to cut the tension I said he could have an extension
on his paper. He said not to worry,
he had a good lawyer from Jacoby and Meyers.
Those of the class who knew better groaned.
"You need a great lawyer," I said.
"An expert in civil suits—you could sue the city.
Just think of the psychological damages
to your family alone." Then someone in the back row
held up The Post, the front page declaring
the jury had acquitted
the policemen who'd beaten Rodney King.
We all knew what we had seen—
yet today's paper seemed less real,

more frightening than the videotape.
I wrote the words irony and metaphor
in big block letters on the chalkboard.
David stood up and bowed,
the best of definitions we could come up with.

CHRIS BRANDT
writer, carpenter, teacher

FOR HENRY DUMAS

Tonight your friends
said your words aloud,
and all that spoke through you
came out of their mouths,
made their hands jump, fly,
point, punch, caress us
in an intimate dance
of head and heart
to your words' beat.

On the subway back downtown
your words still drum
in my belly and heart,
"rain cotton" and valentines,
revel in their own accent,
and dance through tunnels
in old overalls, in tweed jackets,
in robes of bright color,
and naked as water.

Exulting at finding you I turn the page
to find again a bullet,
a cop, a face as white as mine,
and you, shot dead at a Harlem subway stop,
a case of "mistaken identity."

I'm holding the book
your fellow griots have made
of your thirty-four years,
stroking its cover,
like a lover's before a long absence.
My face is not my own.

We'll never hear now
how you'd have told
about that subway stop,
or ever stop that bullet
from taking you off.
But your songs
and the space where your heart went
still will hold us all.

TOM C. HUNLEY

public relations writer

BROOKLYN SOUTH BLUES

Never forget how the cops of the 70th precinct tortured Abner Louima
with a toilet plunger, while they smile and make peace offerings,
while their boots march the other way and don't trample you, when
you start thinking *they've changed, they've changed;*

remember the darkness while the sun keeps burning, streetlamps shoot
their dusty streams, moonlight funnels down and frenzied dancing
keeps the rainclouds away:

in the day when only criminals tremble, and the sweatshops get busted,
and those who look out of the windows see clean streets;

and the doors remain unlocked, and no one remembers the cracking of teeth,

and the broken man's words lodge themselves in the voice of a bird, and
the echo of protesters' voices dwindles away, drowned out by innu-
merable television sets;

and citizens vaguely fear the billy club at the cop's side, and their fears
make them behave in the home of the brave;

and eel grass grows in Jamaica Bay, and hackberries and dogwood fruit
prosper in Prospect Park, and no one is hungry, no one is wary, no
one listens to the bird whose song rises above the darkness;

and editors find new ways to sell newspapers, and memory fails; because
the Internet inundates us with information, causing overload and
amnesia, and mourners die with no one to mourn them:

give it time, keep Abner Louima in mind. Forgive slowly, and never forget.

Become the bird that sees all, sings all. Then the law will be a light again,
and no darkness will forcibly penetrate it.

HAVE YOU SEEN ME

You can't go a hundred in a sixty-five
on a highway you're not paying attention
to the troopers will gun you from behind
fake trees or hidden curves as a grassy
knoll slides down your eye's left side
like Evel Kneivel's landing ramp but that's
exactly what I did and when I saw the trooper
I shot down to eighty but then back up
to a hundred when he started coming I took
the first exit onto a service road where
his car was too fast for my car he got me
the wind blew his hat onto my windshield
just keep a straight face got to keep
a straight face now he's out of his squad
car with a magnum light and that rifle
and I'm nothing to him but his bitch ex-wife
the screaming chief the IRS I shot his partner
fucked his girl I peed in his pancakes boiled
his rabbit spilled his cocaine there's a body
in my kitchen another in the bed I put brie
in them both to attract the rats I'm Happy
the Clown with a kid on my lap I'm Paul
Bernardo Patrick Bateman I go out at night
to dig up earthworms David Berkowitz
before his parking ticket I'm the man it takes
them careers to catch my face in banks
my name in the mouth of hungry dispatchers
cheekbones in the lead of composite sketchers
gait on the film of crossing guard eyes I've
lost this much hair put on this much weight
tattooed the text of APB's on the foreheads
of victims and when this trooper starts
asking me where I'm going so fast I'm going

to ask him where are any of us going officer
sir when it comes down to it aren't we all just
burning to put a face to a name.

DAVID G. EPSTEIN
law enforcement administrator

UNTITLED #2

in the dark
of any night
what do you know of
us?
no—not what
the young reporters and
their agenda-driven editors
have you read.
that we are
bigots
blue collar
sadists
and all white with
red necks.
we know
you know
all this.
do you know what it means to lock eyes with someone who wants
to kill you?
admit it.
you don't have the dimmest spark of recognition
the remotest flicker of
what that means.
you see us
kicking someone who aroused
the adrenaline of fear in us
by going after our lives
and you know all you want to know.
we are brutes.

KEVIN YOUNG

professor

DEFACEMENT { 1983 }

acrylic & ink on wallboard
25 X 30

Basquiat scrawls
& scribbles, clots
paint across

the back
wall of Keith Haring's
Cable Building studio—

two cops, keystoned,
pounding a beat,
pummel

a black face—scape
goat, sarcophagus—
uniform-blue

with sticks. The night
Michael Stewart snuck
on the tracks

& cops caught him
tagging
a train—THIRD RAIL

DANGER LIVE
VOLTAGE—
taught him better

than to deface public
property. Choke
hold. Keep NEW YOKE

CITY Clean.
Give those men
a PABST BLUE

RIBBON, a slap
on the wrist
a meddle

of honor. Basquiat
produces *Beat
Bop*, black

on black
vinyl—VOCAL.
TEST PRESSING.

INTESTINES.
TARTOWN
RECORDS. EAR.

All revolutions
33 1/3.
When Haring moves

up & out, he'll tear
down that wall
careful to get

Basquiat out intact—
in Haring's
bedroom modeled

after the Ritz
¿DEFACEMENT?
sits, saved

like a face, framed—

CORBET DEAN
police officer

ODE TO THE UNFORTUNATE ONES

When I park my police car at 27th and Van Buren,
I swallow the scent of urine
that drips
from the scabbed ones who scatter
across the homeless expressway
of a dirty alley behind Circle K.

Today, as I wander the store, I want nothing more
than endless rows of candy
to separate me
from these people who stare harder
and slowly move farther
from the badge, the belt, and the gun.

Sure, the whispers and glares get wearisome.
but last week I shot Jamel Peetry;

now memories of his death rise to greet me
in the calcified eyes
of a dusty, disheartened boy
about four
who looks up from the floor
to spear a stare straight through me.

I don't know if he can read, but the T-shirt on his back
hangs white letters on black to broadcast the eulogy,

"In memory of Jamel Peetry,
gunned down by the Phoenix Police."

Eventually, the clerk asks me
why I didn't try
shooting Jamel in the shoulder or the arm.

He means no harm,
he's just a civilian who thinks every cop
can move like Mel Gibson:

Hey, I don't roll around on the ground
and blast away,
I can't shoot smiles in paper targets
from a mile away...

but I can communicate truth,
so I look at the clerk as if to say,

   "I was there
   to arrest Mr. Peetry
   after he kidnapped his girlfriend at gun point
   then butt-fucked her til she bled
   and cried.

   Days later,
   inside an inferior place called 'Superior Court,'
   I listened to the lie, 'No victim—no crime'
   explode like a shotgun
   when the same woman refused to testify
   against the father of her son.

   Then last Sunday night, I was the one
   drawn to the woman's screams.
   During an awful dream
   of gun blasts and shattered glass,
   two of us got shot;
   as we both lay bleeding,
   I was the one breathing, but
   Jamel was not."

To my surprise,
the clerk seems to sympathize
by turning away in silence...

Leaving the store, I stop at the door to brace myself:

When I have to look back, I don't count heroes,
just Jamel, the girl, and me:
three
regular people who,
in the time it takes to raise a gun
became two
planets of regret,
two victims of crime
who both need time
to process, and heal.

Yet two years from today,
I will spill my first tears for Jamel in streams
when I pick up the phone and hear his girlfriend say,

   "I still hate cops...
    but thanks for being there
    and thank you for not ignoring my screams."

S.H.U.

So they say he was a long thin man,
    nevertheless they said they could not see him
    through the window. He had simply vanished
    like an idea in a blank mind

    They said they had to run around
    a corner, unlock some gates, and chains,
    it took a while, by the time they found him
He had hung himself. Imagine a body in mid-air
    Nothing to hang from, nothing to hang with
    No rope no tie no hangman's noose, the goose
    is cooked, the man is gone, imagine that.
    In solitary confinement,
under continual surveillance, he disappeared.

    He was a menace, they said. Had escaped once,
    might try again. Had thrown feces at them.
    His teacher said he was a very bright man.
    Crafty and dangerous, they said. Yipping and barking
    like Mohicans heard through European ears,
    they busted in, all six of them,
    covered in riot gear, masks and helmets, flailing
    batons, they dragged him out, and just as
    they said, he was dead.

    A brush fire flitting across their faces, all the way
    out to the gate, that smile of shame.

NONVIOLENT RESISTANCE AND A COW

Firing 43 shots into an animal occurs to me to be unusual.
—Irvine City Manager Paul Brady

Cops put how many bullets into the side
of a runaway cow?
How many shots per stomach is that?

Well, maybe she got surly, maybe
she was armed or pumped
on growth hormones, maybe the poor cops
just needed to vent their aggression on something.

And why was a cow
on the San Diego Freeway anyway?
Who was she in such a hurry to visit?

Couldn't she get a ride? Couldn't she figure out
how to flag a cab or hitchhike? Or
did she just get sick
of the same old world of grass, manure, and barn,
like others who become "dangerous"
when they can't sit in their prescribed niche?

Martyrs speak all languages, I guess,

their spirit can't be bought
by any amount of magic beans as they run naked down freeways,
eyes wide as moons, breathing hard,
lowing out
their brief victory.

FREEDOM OF SPEECH: AN IMPROVISATION BASED ON THE HŪM BOM RHYTHM

Freedom of speech? I'm an average citizen, scared of the cops.
Freedom of speech? I'm an average citizen, scared of the cops.
Freedom of speech? I'm an average citizen, scared of the cops.
That's my attitude. That's my attitude, too!
That's my attitude. That's my attitude, too!
That's my attitude. That's my attitude, too!

In the mid 1970s, Allen Ginsberg began experimenting with spontaneously composed lyrics and poems. "Freedom of Speech" is the first publication of an improvised lyric from a poetry reading at the Naropa Institute in Boulder, Colorado, on August 7, 1976, composed to the rhythmic structure he'd used previously for his poem, "Hūm Bom," in 1971. —Randy Roark

I'M A POET, DAMN IT

How I was run out of New York City for being a poet

I lived on 76th Street near Riverside Drive,
my apartment the size of a Twinkie
with a tiny terrace overlooking the Henry Hudson River.

One night not too late, I performed poetry from said terrace...

rained words down on society, every unassuming passerby
was enabled—no, empowered—hearing my poetry.

I dressed in black and snapped my fingers a lot
bounced my words down to the sidewalk—people
looked up, smiled, waved, laughed or cursed me.

The beautiful women who lived across the street
continued to parade naked in front of the window—
I never knew if it was for my benefit or their own.

There were three of them, all blonde.
I appreciated my view of river and beauty

and that I could poetize spontaneously without combusting.
For a moment, I felt...like a poet, damn it!

This moment seemed to last a lifetime as I hung on
to terraced poetic perfection with my last words—

Suddenly, sirens rifled the night! A huge searchlight scanned
the building searching for outlaws, chasing scofflaws, beam
hunting relentlessly for the words, I left hanging from those walls.

A blue-suited megaphone shouted up into the apartment hierarchy—
YOU, UP THERE!
searching for this disturber of the peace.

The women across the way got dressed
alerting me to the dangers lurking below where
New York's Finest danced in criminal pursuit minuet
to the desperate tune of my best poems.

Disguising myself in a trench coat
I slipped outside without ID, politely
asked the head cop—*What are you doing?*
What's going on—was there a murder?

He shook his head!
Massive manpower assembled on West 76th Street
four cop cars; bubblegum machines blazing
stopped all traffic on the street—my audience dispersed!

The cop with megaphone was serene
going about his business with Dirty Harry mentality,
demanding that I stand down and surrender.
Only I was not there, I stood next to him
devil-may-care, not making his day.

I asked again—*What's going on?*

He replied with Clint Eastwood finality
THERE'S SOMEONE UP THERE TALKING TO PEOPLE WITHOUT PERMISSION,
WE ARE HERE TO STOP HIM!

And you need this show of force to—

HE IS ARMED AND DANGEROUS!

He might be loaded I thought to myself…as
I leaned real close, whispered in his ear:
Oh, he is armed and dangerous, all right

—He's a poet, damn it!

GIL FAGIANI
social work administrator

FESTIVAL ON 102ND STREET

Mothers line up with their kids
in front of an ancient flatbed truck
with twirling cages
spewing black smoke
out of upright exhaust pipes
Women in hand-painted stalls sell
arroz con pollo
fritters, franks
cerveza e bacalaitos
Cops wearing seaweed-green sunglasses
lean against a wooden horse
"What's that shit?"
one of them says
pointing to a pile of *morcillas*
—black blood sausages—
A mob of young people
squeeze into a vacant lot
to hear a local band
shake up the heavy, humid air
with a chorus of four trombones
Muchachas wiggle their fingers, hands and hips
to the boogaloo beat
Somebody rubs against
somebody else's *culo*
a fight breaks out near the stage
Two cops wade into the crowd
swinging their billy clubs
like machetes clearing a path
through jungle underbrush
A man picks himself off the ground
throws a beer bottle
conking one of the blue-suited *macheteros*
The injured cop holds his ear

tears mix with blood
calls in reinforcements
from the 24th Precinct
the troops club another path through the crowd
trombones blowing louder
to drown out the screams, shouts
and feet flying over brick rubble

MAGGIE JAFFE
professor, editor

SACRED LAND

In the aftermath of the uprising,
the *Times*' photo shows cops
dressed to kill, wielding
"nigger sticks" and loving it.
White boys, Young Lords,
caged Panthers, all are
skin-searched, rain-soaked,
hands thrust over head.
Forced to run the gauntlet:
"'Prison power' my ass,
you motherfuckers."
Attica! Gray walls on the green
Tonawanda Reservation, sacred
land stolen from the Senecas.

Where's Governor Rockefeller
and why won't he fly American
to the Rez? He's stuck inside
his secretary with the heart attack
blues again, his pumped-up penis
engorged inside her.
"Get him the fuck out of me,"
she screams, shoving against
his rigor-mortised body as paramedics
break down his penthouse door.

Before he dies, Rocky unleashes his
National Guard: 43 inmates are gunned
down, 89 wounded and 9 guards are accidentally shot.
According to eyewitnesses, Sam Melville
(his *nom de guerre*), imprisoned for his radical
opposition to the Vietnam War,
is intentionally executed
after D yard's subdued
on September 13, 1971.

Who gave the orders?
Who took the weight?
Opened fire on Melville #26124?
Named him "the mad bomber"?
Who napalmed Viet Nam, Laos, Cambodia?

JACK AGÜEROS
workingman

PSALM FOR EQUATIONS

I am sleeping in Detroit, Lord,
And I am afraid
Of this American Town.

The Algiers Motel is here
And I am afraid the dead will ask
"What went wrong, what
Human deed gave such offense, or
Terrified them into a response of fire?"

Lord, you need a new Angel of Equations
Because the dead blacks
Far outnumber
The credible police.

(Note: The Algiers Motel was a welfare hotel where three white police officers shot three black youths to death in 1967.)

MARC LEVY

vietnam veteran

RUDY AWAKENING

Mr. Mayor, in the unlikely event one of New York's finest commands
'Show me some fuckin ID or I'll break your face'
Then hauls off, wraps a nightstick 'round your head, stomps your ribs,
Tags you with assault, please, at all costs you must remain...calm.
Mr. Mayor, please do keep your head should four heavily armed
Undercover men peg you a drug lord hell-bent on cocaine
Shout nothing, then shoot and shoot, the gun-crazed air smoke stunned,
Your arms and lungs, legs and heart exploded in one furious burst.
As decent, law abiding, veteran New Yorkers, we beg you,
Though it defies all logic and common sense, remain absolutely...calm.
Furthermore, in the near impossibility you or yours
Are somehow caught in a reverse buy or sting,
Smartly cuffed, paddy wagoned, booked, printed, strip-searched
By overzealous men, no, do not be alarmed at mauling hands
Prodding, poking, inserted deep in private places,
Drawing down blood. Ahh, mi amigo,
Better cowled human hands than human-fouled wood.
Thus and therefore we the undersigned beg you
In God's great name: Remain absolutely calm.

BRUCE WEBER
art historian, poet

THE VOICE ON THE SUBWAY

your attention please
this train is
out of service
police officers
proceed to car 7
an escaped mental patient
named samantha mcoy
is knocking into everybody
i knew her mother
she used to be
a dancer at roseland
her father operated
the bumper car concession
at coney island
samantha went crazy
after a summer
of free rides
her face dented
her teeth crooked
and
sometimes she mumbles
the melody to auld lang syne
in memory of that summer
knocking into things
her body wanders
like a puppeteer's
pulling her strings
so she ambles
in half circles
searching for her
mother and father's
grave
your attention please

this train is
out of service
police officers
proceed to car 7
samantha mccoy
is bumping into people
tell her she'll be given a big room all her own at bellevue
so she can wander without getting hurt
tell her you'll bring her a compass
so she can easily
navigate the grounds
tell her everybody at the hospital
misses her knocking into them
your attention please
this train is
out of service
police officers
proceed to car 7

MARTÍN ESPADA
lawyer, activist, poet

THE SIGN IN MY FATHER'S HANDS

—for Frank Espada

The beer company
did not hire Blacks or Puerto Ricans,
so my father joined the picket line
at the Schaefer Beer Pavilion, New York World's Fair,
amid the crowds glaring with canine hostility.
But the cops brandished nightsticks
and handcuffs to protect the beer,
and my father disappeared.

In 1964, I had never tasted beer,
and no one told me about the picket signs
torn in two by the cops of brewery.
I knew what dead was: dead was a cat
overrun with parasites and dumped
in the hallway incinerator.
I knew my father was dead.
I went mute and filmy-eyed, the slow boy
who did not hear the question in school.
I sat studying his framed photograph
like a mirror, my darker face.

Days later, he appeared in the doorway
grinning with his gilded tooth.
Not dead, though I would come to learn
that sometimes Puerto Ricans die
in jail, with bruises no one can explain
swelling their eyes shut.
I would learn too that "boycott"
is not a boy's haircut,
that I could sketch a picket line
on the blank side of a leaflet.

That day my father returned
from the netherworld
easily as riding the elevator to apartment 14-F,
and the brewery cops could only watch
in drunken disappointment.
I searched my father's hands
for a sign of the miracle.

COPS & ROBBERS 2

Took four cop cars
and twice as many cops
to bust a car-full of college boys
on a traffic violation
outside my house
Sunday night

Started out
just one shaking cop
　Just doing my job
Pulls em over
Probably ran a stop sign
Going a little too fast
Wanted to know
　　Hey boys, what's going on over here

Cop was scared
You could smell as he shouted
　Stay in the car and put your
　　Hands in the air so I can
　　　See

Afraid of a shoot out
He's calling for back up
To issue a ticket.
Uniforms swarming my street
Over the megaphone yelling
Put your left hand out the window
　　Open the door with your right
　Get slowly out the car
　I said

Got the driver cuffed and spread eagle on the hood
Before you could say
    Have a doughnut or
        Got a problem over here or
        Put your hands in the air where I can see em
Hammers cocked on a couple of
white boys
drunk and scared in the back seat

Asking me to
        Get out of the car
        Nice and slow
    Keep your hands in the air where we can
        see

Cuffed and spread-eagle for running a
stop sign
Thank god it wasn't
black boys or a couple of
cholos
I couldn't have looked out my window
watched the whole thing then
Would have had to take cover
Cops so scared
it shakes the bullets down
the barrel of that
smoking blue light
special

EVIE IVY

dancer

COMPASSION

"For everything exists, and not one sigh, nor smile, nor tear,
One hair, nor particle of dust, not one can pass away."
—William Blake

Going from Brooklyn to The Bronx
The train rattled into a Manhattan
Station as the conductor said, "This
Will be the last stop, everybody out."
"Everybody off," drummed into
Our ears again and again.

I stepped out among mumbling
Riders and soon was chatting
With a woman next to me.
We went from trains, how late
We now might be, to the news
And start talking about those cops

And she says, "I think that the ones
Who did *that* in *that* precinct in
Brooklyn deserve the highest form
Of punishment. But the ones
That did *that* in The Bronx..."
On the crowded platform she's

Lowered her voice to whisper,
"Made a mistake," her skin also
Brown-tinged and a Bronx resident
Who speaks her own thoughts,
"Things happen, things go wrong,"
As the next train pulled slowly in.

It was only an animal…
I remembered once in some precinct
A dog, the mascot was beaten
To death—no split-second decision
Here—for doing what was natural.
I felt the ocean's uproar.

Sometimes another train doesn't come,
And there has to be time to think…

RENE SALDANA, JR.

teacher & novelist

THE NOBLE SPEECH

Based on Gary Fields' article in USA Today *titled "Course walks teens, police down a two-way street," dated Monday, November 15, 1999*

Teens need The Speech
(And more)
To survive into their 20's?

NARRATOR [standing, hands clasped
In what appears to be prayer]:
Don't get out of the car;
If you disagree with the officer,
Say so
Before
The officer begins
To write
[Guilty as sin, Spic/Nigger],
But be respectful.

And more?

Stay calm,
Remain civil,
And don't
[Do *not*, ever, ever,
Even when you're in the right
DON'T]
Make any sudden moves
[Like going for your
License—he thinks gun—
In your back pocket,
A move which will give
License to a cop
To pull his gun
From his holster]

Today, cops'll "Leave the radios, guns
And handcuffs outside"
They say, "Leave your color
Outside," but
Outside we are nothing but our color
And they are theirs

COP [screaming]:
"You know the drill.
Get your hands up against the wall."

ANOTHER COP [feeling against
A wall himself, because within these walls,
He's left "the radios, guns and handcuffs
Outside"]: "You want to be respected...
It's a two-way street."

[Some of those getting
The Speech today
Are impressed by the officer's
Brutal honesty, here, today,
But they have to wonder
"How much of what the chief has said
[Today about two-way streets,
And civility, and respect]
Actually filters down
To the 13,000 officers
In the department?"]

CHIEF [arms crossed]:
"The young officers have to learn...
The young people have to learn..."

KIDS [their own arms crossed,
Wonder still, some
Maybe shaking heads, all of them
Remembering run-ins

With Johnny Law]:
We're here, trying to learn.
Where're they? The 13,000?

ANSWER/NARRATOR:
Out on the streets,
With the radios
Guns
Handcuffs
Ready to show you
Who's really in charge.

JOHN GREY
financial systems analyst

STOPPED BY COPS

You hate being stopped by cops.
You know you've been speeding
but don't feel as if
you've done something wrong.

You detest the way
they make you sit and wait
while their lights
blaze in front of you.
Compared to that
swirling red,
your headlights
are weak and vulnerable.

There's nothing more
devastating in your mind
than when the cop
hovers over you,
asks for identification.
All of you
is squeezed into a tiny license,
a pathetic registration,
while he is everything else,
the darkness, the mountains,
the forbidding shoreline.

The ones you rush away from
or hurtle towards
would never stop you here.
You were over the limit,
is what he's saying.
What he means is,
your life is not your own.

SHERYL L. NELMS
insurance investigator

ARRESTED

is to have ten Ft. Worth cops
crowding through your
front door

shotguns pointed
billy clubs clenched
pistols cocked
cuffs ready

reaching through your legs

grabbing and twisting
your balls

that is arrested

DAVID NIELSEN
production manager

THE STORY SO FAR

then suddenly they leapt from the car, automatic rifles
like the history of all death waving in the air, a bad dream
about to unfurl and they knew it; the men yanking masks
over their faces, the black guys with great gigantic arms,
wristwatches, the white guys with big heads of feathered hair,
sunglasses, everyone in denim, lowering their weapons
on the car in front of them then flinging the doors open
and by the backs of their necks, after having first assured the kids
in the car that they would most certainly kill them if given the chance,
dragged them out of their car and onto the street, face down,
and all traffic had stopped and everyone including myself
took a step backwards; even the bold DEA lettering on their jackets
meant nothing, having never been shot at and not intending to,
although once on a greyhound at midnight in philadelphia
after our power had been cut and the driver was mugged
and the b-boys carrying knives in back leapt to his rescue
outside of the bus, although on that one occasion a latino
b-boy rescuer leapt back on the bus shouting, everyone get off the bus!
they've got guns and they're going to open fire! then suddenly
it was like being on an airplane whose engines have died
and everyone knows they're going to die and as i looked into
the back of the bus i understood panic: suddenly we'd become
like animals crawling over each other, literally shoving each other down,
even children, suitcases ripped open, underwear afloat,
arms akimbo, a fistfight had broken out in our effort to escape
and i remember slumping into my seat, unable to believe anyone
would want to open fire on a bus in philadelphia and wary as hell
of the insane as they fled past me and into the street and into what exactly?
where would they go if some lunatic opening fire on a passenger bus
decided he'd rather shoot a live running target instead? i thought
about that and tried to become like a chameleon blending
into my surroundings or like a twig moth camouflaged
by his coloration or even, if possible, like the air unseen.

but then they brought out guard dogs to sniff the car for crack
and the DEA, having grown bored, took notice of the crowd
around them, their pistols revolving as they revolved to face us,
and i wondered what would happen next.

FELTON EADDY
writer, arts educator

BLACKMAN BROTHERMAN & THE HIGHWAY PATROLMAN

i.

It was a sad, sad funeral as most are—gray
sprinkling spring rain falling softly
on white sandy cemetery
seemed to make it sadder for some
as black hats and founded shoulders
huddled under umbrellas
and branches of tall green oaks
for some it was purification
a blessing from the gods to wash away pain
for Uncle Leon was hard to beat
if he could in fact be beaten by mortal man

he was a social worker before worry
wore down the pulse of his pancreas
up from the belly of South Carolina 'bacco
back fields to New York
in and out of time ticking tenements
a thirty-year man perusing projects
til the first year of retirement
when his body came to rest
in a Carolina grave next to his mother
who had in later years moved to Brooklyn to be in his care

returning to Georgia from his funeral
I headed south on I-95
the Carolina sun beaming brightly into my red eyes
before the junction of I-20(20/20) to Atlanta
streams of white light orange ball aglow
behind thick green pines of the PeeDee
curly Spanish moss waving lazily from oaks
thick like gray afros are memory songs

Blackman, brotherman and the blues
sun glinting down on the windshield
as I drove alone into blinding sunlight
which comes to rest on I-20(20/20) west
about this time in the afternoon
the power of the car, the mood, the moment
made me sit upright
my right foot, right leg, right cheek
relaxed, relieved from the foot pressing firmly
forward to Atlanta.   I had it on *cruise* control

ii.

Wednesday, March 20-something, 5:30 PM
I fumbled with gadgets on my lap—ommmmmm
a pair of silver Chinese balls—ommmmmm
a chanting bell and mallet—ommmmmm
riding down I-20(20/20)
as if the paper mill stench of the PeeDee River
was not warning enough
as I crossed the thick pinebelt draped with
scuppernong and ivy vines.
Mother's Days, weddings, funerals
back and forth on the edge of Swamp Fox City
I have come to bear witness
to what blackman-brotherman
driving the highway has come to know for sure

"Getting Late in the Evening"
bright metal chrome glittered in the rearview mirror
the right-left flash-flash of white blinking lights aglow
Blackman-brotherman and the blues
riding the interstate is no new news
sunset spoiled by the blue bubble-light
a staccato pulsation
rushing the rhythm of my heartbeat

holding sixty-three
in a sixty-five mile per hour zone
radio down low
I had it on cruise control
but the blue, blue, bright lights
of two patrol cars in my mirror

nobody knows the trouble I've seen
I think/nobody knows/the rental/and nobody cares
agreement is in/my heavenly burden/the glove compartment

Carolina sunshine beaming down
burning redneck son of a southern buckra, he said:
"Just come back here,
um on write you a warnin' ticket"
western sun of Carolina
please, oh please, take me home
a warnin' ticket! a warnin' ticket!

iii.

twenty-five years of driving this road
qualifies me, certifies me forewarned.
ain't no new news
Black brotherman and the blues
cruising on the freeway
with a state trooper
riding the highway
but my shoes are too tight
like the hard leather loafers I wore on Easter Sunday
my legs are too stiff
like the stark red face of trooper Hunnicutt
who had cut across the grass median
with the blue light stroking
sending my heart pumping

doom-doom, doom-doom,
doom-doom, doom-doom,
me and trooper Hunnicutt, doom-doom
we stood between the bumpers of our cars doom-doom!
he faced east; I faced west
doom-doom
he wrote the ticket, doom-doom
I held my breath

"And we wanna search your car," he said.
wanna search your car, wanna search your car
"On what grounds, please?"
"Give me your keys!"
"Don't hit me, don't hurt me,
and I want a lawyer present."
"My lawyer's sixty miles away.
We ain't got time to git no lawyer—
we gon' search your car," he said.

Pale-pink trooper Andrew
forced his fingers deep into my right pocket.
"I do not have a gun."
then deep into my left pocket
like a young bloodhound thirsty on the chase.
"I am returning to Atlanta to my wife,
to my friends, my job, my life.
If you don't believe me, call my mother."

iv.

wanna suspect: seek brotherman
wanna arrest: stop brotherman
Blackman, brotherman and the blues
wanna subject: search Blackman
under duress: seize Blackman

trooper Andrew ran his hand delicately under the seats
rifled through the trunk, sniffed the hood
trooper Hunnicutt unzipped my fanny pouch
for clues, for a gun, for a knife,
for all the other reasons white boys like
to put the squeeze on brothers'
balls for *no probable cause*

this is an illegal search
a violation of my civil rights
unnecessary detainment
"There is a small knife in my right pocket.
I do not have a gun.
There is a stone in my left pocket—don't bring it out."

Two nights ago I stood beneath the full moon
in a prayer circle with the family
we are protected by angels
we have received God's blessings
I do not have a gun.
As Shango is my strength
you'll pay for harassing me.
"Have you lost anyone lately?"

"We cannot obtain verification
because their computer is broke," he said
"Just let me have my things;
you can have National Car Rental's car.
No, I do not need a ride.
I am strong.
Why don't you just let me go home?"

V.

I squared my crown upon my head
tossed the backpack over my shoulder

and headed west
springing lightly across the green grass
growing anew along the shoulder
forward into the sunlight's orange glow

Good-bye Hunnicutt; good-bye Andrew
burden laid down by the roadside
and a fourth of a mile away...
"Hey-hey! Hey! Come back," they yelled.

I stopped, and walked back to the maroon Chevy Cavalier.

"You can have your car.
We found the rental agreement
on the bottom of the glove compartment.
You can go," said Andrew, the old 'coon dog.
He tossed the keys across
the top of the maroon Chevy Cavalier.

He spat brown chewing 'bacco
from the corner of his mouth
"What you think
all the police do is beat up on blacks?"

I sipped long on the bottle of spring water
as they drove off into the sunset.
I followed the western Carolina sun
home to Atlanta, GA with one eye
peeled in the rearview mirror.

There are some strange things happening between
Black men and the police.
I don't wanna be a part of it.

INSIDERS

"They'll put you behind bars for that!"

To be put behind bars. Exotic creatures in a human zoo, visible in glimpses only as they walk (or strut or stagger) around behind the gates. Sharing a single environment beyond the bars, two species inhabit the gray stone/black steel skeleton of prison: the guarded and the guards. Everybody's doing time—some full-time, some part-time, but time is time and every swinging dick on the tiers is just another cell in the jailbody. If inmates are the bloodstream and heartbeat of incarceration, the CO's are its T-cells, racing along the stream and looking for problems, as much a part of the anatomy as if they'd been sentenced, rather than hired, to spend their days behind the walls.

Incarcerated time is more dense than free time—it takes longer to struggle through the segments of a day when every rhythm is outside your control. Between the wake-up whistles and sirens of lights-out lockdown are meal bells separated by hours heavy as weeks. Between court dates and parole hearings stretch lifetimes of months. The one thing an inmate has more of in prison than he had on the street is time. All the time in the world.

PHILLIP MAHONY
NYPD

ON GIVING A POETRY READING AT ARTHUR KILL CORRECTIONAL FACILITY

It is not my desire
to forgive,
or theirs
to be forgiven by me.
To understand each other
is more important
and much less pleasant.
It takes courage even to try,
because from up close,
from this close,
one sees that
the walls between us
are not made of stone,
but of circumstance.
We are not as far apart
as we'd like.
How should I begin?
Look the murderer
square in the eyes
and realize:
that too could have been me.

CHRISTOPHER PRESFIELD
inmate

THE GUARD
after Robert Frost

He walks in darkness it seems to me,
one foot square behind the other,
forever turning in circles. Keys
are another thing, big as bacon strips
and twice as useless, as if no wall
surrounded a city of stone. Then
how keeping men in smaller spaces
forever grayer, crowded, and cramped
might truly serve some civic end.
And the fist he holds inside
how it always defines his service
to a public so fey and quick to deny
how duty and heart might follow
the gate they close behind him.

HETTIE JONES
writer & teacher

THE SEMIPERMANENT GATE LIST*

The semipermanent gate list
is dogeared in a looseleaf binder

Semi hardly describes it
you could be disappeared
in an instant, ah! Bye-bye page twenty-five,
        miscellaneous

Unlike the list the gates themselves are fixed
as if forever as they finger you

The intimidation gate
sniffs
your dirty hankie

The keep 'em guessing gate
stamps your hand, infrared
    one week right
    left or right the next

And behind the fear gate's
razor wire grin

are the steel-barred business gates
and keys in the hands of those who get paid

to know you as a piece of paper
blowing up a long empty hill

* *My clearance category at the prison where I work.*

DANNA BOTWICK
prison visitor

GUARDED
(DROPPING DADDY OFF AT JAIL)

Good-bye at the gate
We hugged & kissed like families do
He held his youngest daughter,

She wanted to see where he would sleep.

The guard, a black woman
with sunglasses & white uniform,
scooped up his belongings with
long red nails.
It's just a camp,
no bars, she made light
of our darkness and I hated her
long red nails.

Lucy did not cry
for almost two hours.

When it folded over her,
she was trying to spell
and decided she could not do her work
without him
so she beat the couch
with small angry fists
"I want my daddy, NOW!"
Until she could not breathe,
eyes puffy,
face flushed she raged,

"I wish daddy didn't do that bad
thing in the first place!"

I paused inside my hurt
and suggested,
"He didn't know..."

Too smart for me
she smashed her face into a pillow,
"I'll bet all mothers say that to their children."

COLETTE INEZ

teacher of poetry

PRISON/CLOUDS

Passing the state correctional facility,
a gunner in the gun post.

Hard blue. After flat miles
of cotton, the prison tower startled.

A day of modest happiness marred—
him saying she's said something she hadn't.

Grim, she stares at clouds leaving islands
where they break apart.

Prisoners believe others
share the grace not to be penned in.

Witness to sunlight's captive colors,
released to the line between heaven and earth,

he ends the impasse: "I might have misheard."
Yield, said the road.

COME AND TAKE ME

It happens next week.
A court date.
A probation violation.
Another line of cocaine.
This time there will be no appointed lawyer.
No fancy dance suave solicitor.
Only the beating heart
of a steroid-pumped man of 25
and the sentencing.
He will represent himself.
He is wearing loaned clothes
and a gifted version of the latest cellular.
He'll shut if off for that day.
For the last 6 months it's been the streets.
Shelters at night.
Building enough roofs.
Shingling until the vomit of yesterday is ejected.
Enough money to supply an aging habit.
A couple of months back,
a Hepatitis C admission.
A warning of weak livers.
Fighting the streets daily.
Pocket money from the government
to pay for taxed cigarettes.
They always get back what they give.
They should just give out chips for the casino.
Tired of the unstoned calm.
Smell of fear and ammonia.
Weights clinking up and down
as quickly as an old Tilt-A-Whirl spinning backwards.
There is nowhere to go.
Body begging.
Mind sifting beyond decency.

Your honor,
please take me
for it has become
my home.

MAGGIE JAFFE
professor, editor

C BLOCK
(EXCERPT FROM "THE PRISONS")

They shackle him in a dark-
green van with boarded-
up windows for the crime
of mainlining good
drugs and the American
Dream—that fucked-up twisted
sister, that gap-toothed white
picket fence. Above him, Orion's
dagger's sheathed in a belt of stars.
The guard tower's revolving light
parodies civility in this "machine
invented to change people."

MURIEL RUKEYSER

poet

THE GATES (EXCERPT)

15.

All day the rain
all day waiting within the prison gate
before another prison gate
The house of the poet
He is in there somewhere
among the muscular wardens
I have arrived at the house of the poet
in the mud in the interior music of all poems
and the grey rain of the world
whose gates do not open.
I stand, and for this religion and that religion
do not eat but remember all the things I know
and a strong infant beginning to run.
Nothing is happening.   Mud, silence, rain.

Near the end of the day
with the rain and the knowledge pulling at my legs
a movement behind me makes me move aside.
A bus full of people turns in the mud, drives to the gate.
The gate that never opens
opens at last.   Beyond it, slender
Chinese-red posts of the inner gates.
The gates of the house of the poet.

The bus is crowded, a rush-hour bus that waits.
Nobody moves.

"Who are these people?" I say.
How can these gates open?

My new friend has run up beside me.
He has been standing guard in the far corner.
"They are prisoners," he says, "brought here from trial.
Don't you see?   They are all tied together."

Fool that I am!   I had not seen the ropes,
down at their wrists in the crowded rush-hour bus.

The gates are open.   The prisoners go in.
The house of the poet who stays in solitary,
not allowed reading   not allowed writing
not allowed   his woman   his friends   his unknown friends
and the strong infant beginning to run.

We go down the prison hill.   On our right, sheds
full of people all leaning forward, blown on some ferry.
"They are the families of the prisoners.   Some can visit.
They are waiting for their numbers to be called."

How shall we venture home?
How shall we tell each other of the poet?
How can we meet the judgment on the poet,
or his execution?   How shall we free him?
How shall we speak to the infant beginning to run?
All those beginning to run?

ANDREW KAUFMAN

english professor

FROM THE CINNAMON BAY SONNETS

Mixing the verses of forgotten children's rhymes
in the unending fluorescent light and smoke
is how I tried, off and on, to break the neck
of night two, pacing the main holding pen,

"the Jew guy," "the guy in the jacket,"
to the young thug who crept into my path
to ask if I knew how to open handcuffs.
I don't know why I picked a frayed match

off the floor—I could hardly see straight enough
to fit it into a keyhole, as if that would do
anything, anyway. I could hardly talk,

and a guy came up to say, "We're all stuck
here and some guys are looking at heavy time.
Yo! Professor! We're all sad, can you tell us a poem?"

TAD RICHARDS
teacher

TEACHING IN PRISON

I wanted to tell you about the front gate at Fishkill
(yes, it's iron bars), and how the desk guard
in her boxy, iron-blue uniform,
badge on blue, keys and communications devices
dangling from her squared-off waist,
tests her metal detector.
This is how: as you stand before her,
arms outstretched like a totem,
shoes three feet apart, she flicks
the hand-held unit on, and runs it
over her left breast, and then it squeals.
Her nipple or her heart? But she's not playing,
her eyes deflect as much intimacy
as the nameplate on her shirt front.
Today, she touched it off
with a nonchalant sweep
downward over her belt buckle
before she probed me with its wire loop.
I had plucked myself clean, as always,
of coins, keys, watch, and didn't squeal.

I wanted to tell you about the girls in frocks
that skip along their ribcages, and
the way the breeze
plaits gay cottons and polys around their thighs;
how they smile, and brush back their hair,
how they're fresh-pressed, fresh-minted—
their smiles are high school smiles, nothing between them and prettiness,
their dresses for a picnic, not the time clock
they punch just outside the iron door.

And maybe they've been on lunchtime picnics
with their families, before punching in
for the second shift at Fishkill,
or maybe they have evening plans with boyfriends—
a beer, a walk down by the river—
boys whose hearts will thwack at the panty lines
visible in the sunset through those thin frocks,
or dance to the crueler beat of foreknowledge.

Those dresses are not for work,
certainly not at Fishkill.
The girls wave their fingers to the desk guard,
and disappear down the hall to change.

I know there is a room down there, with lockers
—no different from a girl's gym
and yet I see it with the heart's incandescence
for being in the heart of Fishkill Prison;
those pretty girls
with blonde hair swept back, dark ringlets, sandy clouds,
eyelashes blooming to the dimensions of pride,
taking their pretty frocks off,
their open-toed sandals,
putting on blue twill pants
without waists or hips or bottoms
closing shirts as heavy as iron doors over their breasts,
sealing the closure with their names, and the name of
the New York State Department of Corrections,
walking out to their stations in heavy black shoes.

These are the wrong stories,
but you must understand I have no enemies here.
The guards smile at me, and I smile back,
gates pop open as I show the card with my picture
head-on, unsmiling, in a white fisherman's sweater
(it was taken in the room where they process new arrivals;
next to the camera is a box of letters and numbers).

Should I tell you, then, about the way the sky looked
my first time in the yard,
the depth of its clarity?
It was 5:30, and winter.
The sunset had withdrawn,
no purple left, no rose, no crimson,
a deep blue glowing through a darker blue
as if blue had finally been revealed
as the ultimate secret of the cosmos.

The sky is always beautiful over Fishkill Prison,
beautiful over Downstate Prison.
Always.
And so big! The low buildings,
the rolling yard, the razor wire fences
make a space that demands such a panorama to cover it all.
The beach doesn't take so much sky,
the prairies of Wyoming,
the Badlands of the Dakotas.
Maybe only the ocean.
All that sky,
to cover a prison!

You tell me that at Greenhaven,
built like a dungeon,
the walls are so high
that the sky is only a pocket.

But what do we have to do with space?
Classrooms are all the same size,
cells are all alike.
What does the sky matter between us?

Listen: if I were sure that what I don't know
was more important than what I do know,
I suppose I'd try to learn the one and forget the other.

REX PRYOR

corrections administrator

SLOW NOTES, FOUND RHYTHMS

they move slow 27 days in the state pen
and they already know there is no hurry
they, them, and it will be there when they
arrive whatever time that may be
sure enough they move faster to chow
it is scheduled at a time to begin and a time to end
they know there are no exceptions for that call
they move slow to stay in the new breeze for as long
as they can cause once they enter the massive house
it's lock up time no skating on the walks
one con told me once
its music man like a song these convicts
slow notes drudgingly moving across
the prison at all different scales
but call chow and they find rhythm movement
slow notes, found rhythms
  it is a song
  it is a song

MAGGIE JAFFE

professor, editor

ULTIMATE APHRODISIAC

Riot. Lock down. The guard—
gray gun-metal eyes and serial-killer
smile—barks, **who started this?**
Twelve hands go up. **Twelve
days in the hole.**

Who didn't? Fifteen hands
reach for the overhead pipes.
Fifteen days in the hole.

He beats his nightstick with a pulsing
rhythm against his thigh, all the while
softly moaning, **I'm getting hard,
man, getting hard.**

WILLIAM HLADKY
detective

DEAD MAN WALKING

Dead man walking,
as grandmother and aunt brace
his collapsing body
at the front door.

Dead man walking,
as he surrenders
to a dozen detectives
at his ghetto hiding place.

Dead man walking,
eyes showing the shock
from knowing that this town this time
won't spare him.

Dead man walking,
high-decibel anguish
from family members
who know too
and who lay hands on him for the last time
while cops escort him away handcuffed.

Dead man walking,
because during a botched robbery
he shot and killed a Dutch tourist.

Dead man walking,
because Miami becomes a vindictive
bitch
when it defends its billion-dollar tourism mill.

Dead man walking,
as the news media shriek
and local politicians pound the ground
like alpha apes
proclaiming the capture
to seduce back
fearful guilders, marks, francs, pounds, lire.

Dead man walking,
for the sixteen-year-old
took his first step out of that apartment
toward the electric chair.

Dead man walking,
because he didn't
kill
a local.

J. DAVIS WILSON
toddler teacher & painter

COMMENCEMENT

My lover and I, righteous
free speech from a public pulpit,
HURWITZ CUTS TREES LIKE HE CUTS JOBS.
My partner and I sit, gray by gray,
jailbird lovers, "criminal trespassers"
jailsupport numbers match on forearms.

We touch knees, flirt.
Strengthen connection, soon
to be separated. Yet, even
in jail, our flames mingle.

A box of repressed, ornery men, gray,
drool on small square windows, eyeing
our every move, hawks on mice.
I can only imagine what perversion
they'll report about me, invaded.

Sensuality escapes from my anus
during animalistic strip search.
My first hearty taste at civil disobedience
cannot be surrendered so easily.

My gray lover, face granite, and I,
snickering in my strut, secretly smile.
Picturing picketers, blocked boat
and solidarity banner exclaiming
truth for workers, CEO's and trees.

I ask the white-haired cop,
busy booking me
if he likes his job...?
    It's something to do during the day,
he replies—as he mutters
    about not doing any reprints today.

"Well, they don't work you overtime
too much, do they?" I implore,
"Oh, yes, they do."
turning to face a pink
malfunctioning computer.

C.O.

For someone like me, not born in Vermont
I don't build stone walls, I don't service the skiers
I paint—I have since sixteen
learned from the oldtimers when I started
with nothing
I'm fast, I'm clean, I work long hours,
you have to stay in this business.
Give me a solid-built New England farmhouse
I'll restore it to the beauty it had in its youth:
the gables the trim the gaunt weathered siding
I have boxes of photos, before and after, for proof

And I'm tall, I save hours on the ladder
with my reach, and I'm strong
I go sunup to sundown,
you have to keep ahead of the shadows of winter,
keep one jump ahead of the snow.
All my gear in a panel truck, the lettering mine,
Scott Miller Paints, yes I do,
word spreads when you're as good as I am,
my name is my payroll
my health insurance and retirement fund.

But take this past winter, my wife and a kid,
two bright dry days between October
and April, the kitchens ran out
the Dairy Queen ceilings, the basement
renovations, we still have to eat.
A state job is the best you can hope for,
my name on that list for two solid years.
When it hit it was my time in the army
that brought the job home, Correctional Officer
in Saint J.'s, a medium state prison.

From detailing windows I'm counting heads
every half hour now, my logbook entries
what I do for the paycheck, regular thank God,
the coin of my realm a compassion I am
trying to keep, but some of these guys
I don't envy their choices, I'll have
two years before I can transfer out,
this place could use a real scrape and paint job!
My rounds at night, the sleep check. The cigarettes
one after the other, their bodies sprawled out,
I'm locked in, too.

W.S. MERWIN

poet

PLEA FOR A CAPTIVE

Woman with the caught fox
By the scruff, you can drop your hopes;
It will not tame, though you prove kind,
Though you entice it with fat ducks
Patiently to your fingertips
And in dulcet love enclose it,
Do not suppose it will turn friend,
Dog your heels, sleep at your feet,
Be happy in the house.

No,

It will only trot to and fro,
To and fro, with vacant eye;
Neither will its pelt improve
Nor its disposition, twisting
The raw song of its debasement
Through the long nights, and in your love,
In your delicate meats, tasting
Nothing but its own decay
(As at first hand I have learned).

Oh,

Kill it at once or let it go.

KATHLEEN ADAMS
arts administrator & teacher

LAST NIGHT IN FILM CLASS

We watched "Clockwork Orange"
and ate pizza,
six large pepperoni
and three medium cheese
bought with moving money.
Ultraviolence.
Officers float
back and forth
on the other side
of the closed classroom door,
up and down
gray, two-tone halls.
I am afraid they will cancel
our film,
carried under my arm
past officers who do not know
who Burgess is.
Later we talk about violence
as ideology,
finish the last slice
of cheese
and bag of chocolate
smuggled in.
Twix and Almond Joy—
what you can't get
in the canteen.
When it's over,
candy wrappers
back in my backpack,
the officers leave us alone.
I hug each of you
goodbye—
first and last time

we cross the line of touch.
Hold on to your lives.
We count pencils to hand back
to the officers,
collect trash cans for the janitors,
walk down the hall
past toilets
sewing machines
and holding cells.

DREAMERS

Cops lie down on makeshift street beds and wake up in another life. Their guns become beings with wants, needs, a voice; their uniforms are stripped away; they are hugged and sucked, comforted and cursed, identified solely by their styrofoam cups. Famous and infamous police actions are rewritten. Cops are compared to swinging doors. They arrest the trees. There are only three of them left. One speaks with a statue.

The poets here have lifted off, left the cities, entered their dreams of what could be or could have been, unfettered by facts. Anti-eyewitnesses, luxuriant with flight. Unsurprisingly, no police officers are represented in this section; the gravitational pull of the job may be too great for them to take off in this way—their study of interiors must be completed first, and there is much work yet to be done there.

KEVIN FREY
teacher

HE LOOKS THE OTHER WAY

On the beat, beside the abandoned
Rug warehouse, he spots the sleeper.
Blankets tossed over plastic pallets.
Garbage bags full of soda cans
And discarded clothes. A beat-up stroller.
A ragged doll, one leg tucked
Beneath the other, perched on the ledge
Above the makeshift bed, watching.
He decides not to roust the guy.

Later that night, on his way back
To the station, the bed is vacant.
Something prompts him to lie down,
Maybe the emptiness of the space,
Maybe his sore feet, maybe the shit
That's long been weighing him down.
Before the early morning light,
Rats scurry away with the ticket book
And leather belt. A raccoon takes
The shiny badge back to its den
In the park. Feral cats shred
The hat, which jays and pigeons
Use to feather their nest. Roaches
Lick crumbs off the undershirt.
A stray dog fetches the nightstick,
Chews it up like an old bone.
A passing shower sweeps the gun
Down a storm drain. The uniform
Shrinks to fit the doll, who
Puts it on, uncrosses her legs, sits
Upright, watches ever more closely
What passes for violence in the street.

Woken up in the morning with a kick.
"Move it along, buddy." And he does.
To the station, the routine, the waiting,
In some strange city where you can't tell
What you'll be when you close your eyes.

MICHAEL CONROY-HARRIS

educator & performer

SECURITY AND PEACE

i want to be held for forty-eight hours
tenderly, by the police
no questions asked, no lies told
just security and peace

i want to be arrested
by their heartbreaking honesty
and tell them it's okay to cry
my cell is your cell, brother
we all fuck up badly sometimes

i want to read my rights
in the eyes of the guys
and the girls as they slip
out of the uniform of their illusions
away from the way of the whip

i want to help them with their enquiries
as long as their questions are right
like 'am i really a gang-member?'
and 'why do I feel at home in the night?'

look at the good cop/bad cop's brain
fried in booze and isolation
i want to help him throw away the keys
and demolish his police station

i want to be held for forty-eight hours
and smuggle in the means of release
safe in the strong arms of ex-offenders
who have woken from their dream of police

and when they hand in their weapons
and turn their backs on their crimes
and stand in the sun on the streets
and say that they're going to start over again
they'll have security and peace

COP

He dreamed that a policeman
stood over him with a club
to make sure he didn't get a hard-on.

Getting control over it
had been his life's goal
back in those schooldays
when the greatest humiliation
was being called to the blackboard
with his pants sticking out
and the boys in the back row snickering,

or getting one
in the crowded showers of the gym,
where to follow the impulse in the hand
he knew would be suicidal—

as in the dream
if he reached out
and groped the cop.

DOUGLAS ROTHSCHILD
editor & teacher

MISSING IN ACTION

So, you're walking toward
the corner of MacDougal

& West 4th Street
just south of the Park

& there's a mounted
cop at a payphone,

his light blue helmet
resting on the top

of the phone's protective
shell. Imagine the conver-

sation: "I don't know; I
only got off it for a second,

where would a horse
go in this town?" & i

think that perhaps i'm
writing a poem by Anselm

Berrigan.

A CURSE ON THE DENTON COPS, THE LOT OF THEM

May you, on your bike patrols be slowed and toppled
    by sand, and let the metaphor of time be gritty in your teeth.

May your own hand (your ticket hand) terrify you
    like a hanky out of nowhere, clean and white.

May you guard the food table
    outside a fiction reading in Ohio somewhere.

      May your seatbelt cut you at the armpit
        and at the topmost gut ripple may you itch like fire.
          May each hive take the shape of a miniature Ohio.

May the Fry Street goth mock your sloth.

May duct tape melt in your hands and be of no use.

May you ogle partygoers, not being one,
    and may they then ignore you like an empty water pistol.

May a sick chicken peck at your shined shoe
    and may your partner in ticketing say, "In Texas or just about any state,
      I suspect that's a bad omen."

May you know you are the pawn of a sad petty empire.

May you have only feminists to console you.

May you be demoted. May you bleat like a sheep in your sleep.
    May you eat week-old lunch meat.

May you never comprehend a poem.

May a poem never describe you
    except to say your hand smells a ticket.

LAW & ORDER

If you watch enough television
You can tell whether or not
You're watching a cop show
By whether or not
The actors are walking around
Drinking coffee from white styrofoam cups
Which seem small in their huge hands
Or have them balanced on the dashboard.
Someday, cops will not need to present a badge
When arriving at the scene of a crime or an accident.
Instead they will hold up their styrofoam cups.

DONALD LEV
writer

A DATE WITH OFFICER BELDING

from the expression she wore
she was sore
at the computer
who bore
our paths to this
point
but she was resigned to do her duty

i, on the other hand, was
overwhelmed by her
patriotic beauty

but the thought of her being trained
in karate,
her black garter belt,

somewhat restrained me.

ours was to be, obviously,
a restrained relationship.

STEVE ANDERSON

lecherous bystander

MOST WANTED MAN

I'm craving for a ploddy
with a body that commands
Come to bed. A private dick
with stick, bomber jacket
and well-hung ammo pouches.

I want to lay it on with the law
wearing his stiff peak,
hot-pressed serge,
with an easy zip
or button fly.

Not a slobby but a bobby
in a smooth thin shirt
with epaulette tongues,
iron thick thighs
and throbbing nightstick.

Cuff me to your cruiser
you big bruiser cop.
Lay down the law
as I lie on the floor
spread-eagled.

SONYA HESS
retired horse whisperer

LIFE OF A POLICE LOVER

1.

Thrown over the lamp
your blue shirt creates false night.
A citron moon burns through,
illuminating the hand, the nipple,
the wet parts gorged with love.

Starry black, your shoes step forward
under the wooden chair
where your holster hangs.

The bullets expand at the thought of flesh.

All night the town fires
flashy outbreaks at us
through the window. I wonder
what we'll do if nothing outlasts
the shirt, the night, the leather.

2.

We walk out pale as prisoners
from the closed bailiwick
of sexual darkness.
The bars' mark still burns
on my spine.

You look at me over
the day's huge glass table
to see what game I play.

We take our first step
without touching.
The Chief reads us our rights;
they are few.

Above us, the sky
is a lucite bowl
swarming with badges.

3.

Shades wrapped around tired vision
you patrol the hard mica garden.
Each morning, the same route.
When you enter my house there's the sound
of rain. We wash together in the last
of summer, letting the ashes run off.

A long pause settles into one drop.

No one may see the red mask
drawn across your skin.
Not the merchants, nailing up
their alarms, or pickpockets scattering
purses or gunmen crouched around corners
with their armpits turning to slag.

Finally, it's November. You cruise
the parks, rain drips through
cold green resin. Your buddies
loosen their belts toward the suave
winter piped through the walls.

I keep busy
puttying the starred glass
back into my shattered windows.

TONY MEDINA
poet, professor, activist

LANDSCAPE WITH USUAL SUSPECT
(on my way to Detroit)

Looking down
From the plane

Chicago streets
Carved into cornrows

Or Bantu knots:
A giant Christmas tree

Spread eagle
Like a dark suspect,

Profiled and usual,
With a cop's foot

On its back
Wrapping itself

Around the city

We cut our way
Through shrouds

Of icy air
Flying into daylight

Staring down
At the snowy gauze

Of Indiana

CHARLES FISHMAN
poet & teacher

WHEELER AVENUE

Amadou Diallo was killed at 1153 Wheeler Avenue on February 4, 1998 by four NYPD officers dressed in civvies. Forty-one shots were fired, and 19 hit their mark.

In 1948, I didn't know we had all been sliced
into races. Wheeler was my block, 1145
the two-story walk-up where my family lived.
I didn't know it was the Soundview section
of the Bronx or that the Bronx wasn't Brookline.
There was no yellow crime-scene tape, only yellow
& white chalk marks on the gray sidewalk.

1145 kicked like a nightstick when Amadou died
a few potsy-steps from Bruckner: on a clear winter
midnight, memory couldn't help him survive.
I want to speak of his crime: how he stood in that red-
brick doorway & couldn't find his tongue, how he knew
no words would help him, that nothing he could say
in the blinding light of four drawn guns would sound like

I am a man, & this is where I belong.

MARC PIETRZYKOWSKI

student, reader, odd-jobist

NOT ON MY BEAT

He put his hand on my knee and all I could think
Was that each morning he woke wanting to sob,
Knowing this world did not want him, and no one in it felt any less—
And at once I knew that this was exactly as it should be, and as he moved
His hand up my thigh, I smiled, and yanked
At the pistol lazing in its holster, pulling at the trigger
So it fired up under the lip of his right kneecap,
And then I kicked open the door and ran up the alley into the light
Of the pharmacy window.
Really what happened was I let him unzip my pants
And put my penis in his mouth, and when I ejaculated
Into his throat, he lifted his head and spit my semen into my ear;
He threw the door open and said "get lost, faggot,"
And I wandered up the alley into the light of the old bait shop.
Oh well, what really happened was I saw
This cop throw a wino up against a car and frisk him, and as I watched
His ass and biceps and back wriggle and twitch from my window
On the second floor, I masturbated
And thought about how it would taste
To have my tongue in the hole at the back of his neck which I punched in him
With an apple corer.

MICHAEL HOERMAN

arts advocate, ex-con

THE COP GUN

for Jimmy Stevens, shot dead by a cop gun, December 1986

The Cop Gun is hungry to erupt
His eyes glaze over like in a dream
If he touches the trigger the Cop Gun shoots
It erupts like a nocturnal emission

When he wakes there is wetness in his shorts
The cop feels guilt
He struggles to justify what has been done
He vows never to do it again

But there are problems with this
He has been given many bullets
He has been given a badge
He sees these as wink and a nod

The cop is turned on by this sick flirtation
He forgets the shame of the wetness
The Cop Gun is hungry to erupt
His eyes glaze over like in a dream

STEVE DALACHINSKY
superintendent

COPS CARE

cops care
like candles off &
on like
coffee breaks
& fountains in winter
& general repairs
or fuel injection

like doctors
& neighborhoods &
swinging doors

cops are
dead bolts &
parliament an
unb~~r~~o ken
chain

cops care
like gladiators &
old tires &
yawns &
         smiles   &   screams.

COLETTE INEZ
teacher of poetry

SLUMNIGHT

T.V. gunning down
the hours
serves as sheriff
in a room
where one yawn
triggers off another,

sends time scuffling
into night.
Wars slugged out
on vacant lots
sign an armistice
with sleep.

Turned to a wall,
the children dream
and the moon pulls up
in a squadcar.

ERIC YOST

no prior convictions

THE DAILY NEWS

Police shoot people for not being police
because we live in a store only salesclerks can shop,
because only trash haulers get their garbage removed,
because only doctors receive urgent medical care.
Okay, that's not true.
Police shoot people for not being police
because only felons have a passion for guns,
because only accountants balance checkbooks,
because only musicians hear melodies,
because only librarians learn how to read.
Okay, that's not true.
Police shoot people for not being police
because a good life must be difficult,
because difficulty makes us happy,
because happiness is always a curse,
because curses encourage harmony.
Okay, that's not true.

COP & ROBBER (SONG)

Officer:
    gadgeted with manacles, et cetera
    beneath that costume
    layered cloths like crimes hide
    usual fallibilities.

    Know the parts?
    Guard the robber
    prompt a smiling
    mask in his pocket
    you won't let him reach for.
    He wears a glass coat.

You missed the cue
in his navel.

NIGHTMARE 9

Keep moving said the cop. The park closes at nine keep moving
dammit. God damn things you think you own the park.

Not talking huh not going noplace? We'll see. Send you up for
observation a week of shock will do you good I bet.

And he blew his whistle.

Whereupon white car pulled up,
white attendants
who set about their job without emotion.
It wasn't the first time they'd seen a catatonic tree.

EDMUND PENNANT
school principal, retired

FORENSIC

They are the last three cops, yes, three,
left in the polis. What can they do
without detectives, fingerprint men?

Even so, they stare at the bare back,
the young, violated back, diagramming
knifemarks, counting the total.

The still-open eyes are slightly crossed,
as in puzzlement or dismay at a nightmare
survived many times simply

by waking from it, which now
she could not do, or remember if, dreaming,
she may have spoken an inflammatory name.

But what's the use when legions of killers
are at large and the TV public are welcomed
to join in the guessing game with no winners.

In a once-great city that has gone broke and
can't afford police, what else can you do
but advise the public to keep their eyes

averted from the stare of strangers with
purposeful glances. What else but to set
the record straight, while dreaming of

a future when a passerby might safely ask:
"Excuse me, haven't we met?" which is a way
lovers used to meet in the good old days.

JIANQING ZHENG
university professor

FIRST SIGHT

after the picture by Grey Villet

At fish-belly daybreak,
a patrolman walked
into the Central Park
in New York City
and was taken by a statue
unveiled the night before:

a humanized Venus
smiled at him, naked
like out of a morning bath,
her left arm akimbo,
her right one lifting high
to wave "Good morning"
to the man who strolled on
pouting his mouth...

TONY MEDINA
poet, professor, activist

LONG DAY'S JOURNEY

O.J. is holding a can of tuna to his head. He's in the back of the white Ford Bronco, threatening to take his life. The cellular phone rings off the hook. Rodney King is driving and, if it were not for the 40 in his one free hand, he'd slam the phone down hard on the receiver to kill the ringing. It is suspected that Jimmy Hoffa's in the trunk. But we are reminded that a Ford Bronco has no trunk. So we figure the foul smell is coming from the glove compartment. Then we hear the weird pop and fizz and don't want to believe that some one as famous and admired as O.J. could emit such a powerful and obnoxious odor. We tried to sneak a glance his way and were relieved to find that it was just the can of tuna split open in the vise grip of his nervous, clumsy King Kong palm. Tuna water dribbled down to his elbow as he sweated profusely, praying that the split open can would not cut his pretty face. When this is all over, I still want to be able to get a job, he told us. Just above our heads propellers chop away at the air. A helicopter lands on the roof of the car. Come out with your hands up! comes the cry from a bull horn. Jimmy Hoffa, sautéed in John F. Kennedy's blood in the glove compartment of the white Ford Bronco, suddenly turns into James Cagney. He is animated. *Ooooh...You'll never take me alive...Ooooh!* Rodney King takes the 40 of Mad Dog and douses the hood of the car, flicking his cigarette out the window to make a fire just in case they send S.W.A.T. men down onto the hood. The helicopter is immediately engulfed in flames, the S.W.A.T. team trapped in a flying open furnace. It hurls away into a ball of flames, shooting out like a meteor, landing like a godsend in Compton, its parts to be picked away like meat off a turkey bone at a homeless shelter on Thanksgiving Day. Rodney King continues to drive, tapping the bottle for leftover drops. Jimmy Hoffa roasting on a spit in the glove compartment. The heat from the hood of the car basting him. Damn! Smells like ribs in there, King groans, fussing with the doorknob of the glove compartment. He loses control of the white Ford Bronco, crashing across guard rails. O.J. nicks his face with the blade of the split open can of tuna. *Fuck!* he yells, blood spraying all over the inside of the white Ford Bronco. Miraculously enough, we end up in front of O.J.'s house on his front lawn. The car engine is dead. It grows cold inside. Ice starts to form on Jimmy Hoffa's body parts. Cops spring out from everywhere: behind bushes, parachuting off the roof, vehicles skidding up onto the lawn, blocking us in. Within minutes we are in My Lai. I awake to find myself in the glove compartment, shivering. Jimmy Hoffa lies next to me sautéing in the blood of John F. Kennedy, smelling of day-old tuna. Outside, King is dragged out the driver's side of the car. Hundreds of cops appear, turning his head into a percussion instrument as nosy pedestrians begin a euphoric rhumba off the sounds the knight sticks make against his skull. The cops continue this until they capture the rhythm of the crowd's dancing. By the time I stick my head out of the glove compartment of the white Ford Bronco to see what's happening, O.J. is whimpering because no one's paying attention to him. (People no longer cared whether or not he pimp-smacked a Barbie doll in a window display case at FAO Schwarz.) His large frame broken down into an endless bouquet of sobs. His tears overflow the can of tuna, flooding the car and raising the temperature while Jimmy Hoffa melts away into John F. Kennedy's blood until a pool of it spills out onto the lawn, washing away the dancing euphoric crowd as Rodney King is being lifted up onto the hood of the car with knight sticks. For a second, in mid-air, just before hitting the trunk, he looks like the good thief, or the bad thief (both of whom stood on either side of Christ on the cross), or Christ himself, innocently pleading, trying not to look surprised when they begin to douse him with gasoline and press a cigarette into the air.

Off in the distance, people will steal TVs and stereo equipment from O.J.'s house. No one will go near the refrigerator.

THOMAS GUARNERA

recent aarp member

PLEASE STAY INSIDE YOUR CAR!

I am sorry, Officer.
So very, very sorry.
> *So sorry I must wrangle*
> *with a baby-face like you.*
> *Where was I when you exchanged*
> *your diapers for a uniform,*
> *your rattle for a gun?*

Trust me, I did not intend
to flaunt the laws of our fair state.
> *Like you flaunt the laws of Adam,*
> *you reject from "Adam 12"!*
> *All lives are lived in between.*
> *They are not red; they are not green.*
> *We have to squeeze the yellow light.*
> *It is not wrong, it is not right—*
> *that's just the way things are.*

A moment's lapse in judgment:
distance, time, velocity.
Have a heart. No harm done.
It could happen to anyone.
> *Even snot-nose punks like you.*
> *Only count the big mistakes.*
> *Like that mistake you made, so young,*
> *swearing allegiance to "the rules"*
> *because they were all you knew.*
> *You will never learn the truth*
> *from inside an armored car,*
> *shielded from uncertainty,*
> *no challenge to your mantra:*
> *"Do not shoot the messenger*
> *just itching to shoot you first."*

Officer, you have my word!
Warn me once and I'm reformed.
Come on, don't throw the book at me.
Give the old man a second chance.
Remember, someday, you'll be old—
the only law that no one breaks.
It's not too soon, not too late,
for learning how to bend.

ROBERT DUNN

assessor

THAT'S MY LUCKY NUMBER?

After hearing forty-one poets
Read forty-one poems
About those forty-one bullets,
I long for the day
Every mother's son of us
Runs out of ammo.

MAGGIE DUBRIS
paramedic, writer, musician

TOILERS OF THE SEA (EXCERPT)

I. He who is Hungry is not alone

I come with my secrets into this strange land of dreams. Look. There's the
Carburetor, there's the siren, there's the stretcher. We're all family
Here. The world is constantly shaking off light. Cutting away a patient's clothes.
Fixed in the glare of a camera.

A lot of things get mixed up in my mind. The names of the skels.
Patrick Gonzalez Bernstein. Jean Paul DiMarsailles. Gone now.
I think dead, but with bits of their light caught in my memory.
"I'm going to get you a diamond ring, Girlfriend," Jean Paul said
On Christmas day. Drunk, with snow in his ears. "You watch and see,
The next time you pick me up, I'm going to give you a diamond ring."

I worked with a medic who had a crazy pet monkey, his wife couldn't handle
It, she called the board every night, we had to drive by the building where
He lived and he went upstairs, taking the radio, taking off all his clothes
In the hallway because the monkey couldn't stand clothes. If we got a call
He would put his clothes back on and come down.

Light drains into my mind like a genie into a bottle. Sometimes I look
At a stove, and I see a woman in a housedress, her head jammed into the
Tiny space between the oven and the floor, her dress crooked across
Her thighs. I hear the cops arguing over her, debating whether this
Might possibly be a natural death. Sometimes, I just see a stove.

II. The Monster

There were good times too. I can't complain.
Parked on the pier, looking out at the Hudson River
With the Chinese fishermen, their white plastic buckets
And the kids from the welfare hotel on 42nd Street
Sitting all the way out on the end, throwing twinkies to the ducks
And the rush of the cars on the West Side Highway, headed home.

The radios were always on. The EMS dispatcher passing out sick jobs and
Men down, the police responding to disputes, robberies, GLA's. The waves
Slapped against the old soggy pilings, the voices went on. The summer of '92.
I lay on the hood of the ambulance, the heat from the engine warming my back
Watching the sun fall between my boots.

There were holes in the pier where the wood had collapsed, and she
Lined up along the south end, built from blankets, plywood and old police
Barriers. We knew all the men that lived there. Shay with his dogs,
Angelo, who claimed to be spending the summer in America as a respite
From his stressful life as an Italian bigwig. At two in the morning,
When the calls slowed briefly, we would drive out again, past the
Crackheads the rats running in the tunnel of our headlights, out to
Where ducks floated dreamy black on the black water, and Angelo and Shay,
Sitting in two ratty old lawnchairs, were drinking and watching the carlights
Race across the Jersey hills.

JOSEPH BROOKE
rancher

KEVLAR CITY

Gazing down the v of a pistol sight, gray iron and smoke and
a smile, power, absolute finality and correction of a
character flaw draws facial tics like a grin of a bad boy
gone right on the brass button circuit. Kevlar,
hollowpoints, chrome bracelets and an attitude necessary to
exist along with garbage left abandoned on the street, on
the automatic vein popping reality of a heroin rush, or meth
jag or a dude tripping near the truth and lies of a TCP
bender, where .357, or .9 millimeter, or .45 split on the lead
tip means nothing except a temporary detour on a journey
fueled in octane madness, a zany killer intent on rape and
harm and homicide and unstoppable except from the courage of
a cowboy sheriff holding the line against instant memories of your own
death. Sure, baby we know, it ain't gonna happen to you, a
jack, a rip, a slice, a red razor of a lifer smelling his
five minutes of fame and wild freedom while paroled from
hard times at Attica. Que bueno, a...say what...tranjillo
baby...close those blue orbs, sleep like a child in hazy
dreams, bash the man, he pumped that black Haitian red in
lead and four crazed Bronx dicks reloaded, did it again.
Man, but it's shadowy in the gutter, in the alley, in the
cesspool where the vermin teem and reproduce and make it bad
for the high percentage, invisible tios and tias and niggers
and spics and chinks and the ground water people who see 9
to 5 and their babies cooing as a reason to make a country
on fire run from top to bottom and not ignite further into a
fireball of racial indignity that could crash the tepee of
cards down upon us all. Sure man, cops, tin badges make
mistakes, see the email of their widows' tears, of the phone
banging at 2am and a frightened police boy's wife's fingers
shaking, hovering over the phone, not knowing if its a wrong
number or a mortician calling with the final news. Easy, no
way. Bad guys, sure, they got blood and DNA and skin and

minds; necessary, you better fucking believe it. Perfect,
naw, but what is. You better fall sweetie, on those luffa
knees, and pray these gals and guys hold that line, that's
right, Tex Mex, Afro America, Chineseola, red men and every
color thereafter, oh yes, cops, they come in all colors,
just like the average Americans they bust their asses every
night in serving. I hate their guts, I love them, I despise
and adore them and I can't imagine how they do it, and can't
imagine life without them. Christ man, I'm just glad it's
them and not me.

AFTERWORD: POST-TERROR

The morning of my 44th birthday was so spectacular weatherwise that I forgot to be pissed off about having to go to work. An hour after I showed up at the office, my birthday was made irrelevant—perhaps permanently so—by the blast and collapse of the Twin Towers. In the following weeks, our smoky city filling with flags and candles as we tallied the missing and canonized the rescue workers, I recognized that *Off the Cuffs*—in process since the spring of 2000 and nearly complete—would have to be placed on hold. Worlds had been reshaped: skylines, attitudes, habits. All our cops were heroes; all perpetrators came from overseas.

Between the slow-burning fire in the World Trade Pit, the regular evacuations of other landmarks (the Empire State Building, Grand Central Terminal, even Penn Station), and a series of anthrax-inspired mailblocks, New Yorkers lived in a state of siege while the unthinkable slipped—slowly, daily—into common history. By October, framed photos of the intact towers had become standard fare on vendor tables throughout the city while art directors frantically airbrushed the twins off the skylines of unreleased movies. As different as these two forms of response appear to be, at root they share the conviction that everything has changed, nothing is what it was before 9/11/01, all scripts must be rewritten.

But I do not agree that every aspect of American life must now be recast in the dust of the trade center. The subjects that concern this book—order and chaos, power and powerlessness, guilt and innocence—are vast categories into which the terrorist attacks must be absorbed and from which they may be interpreted, not subsets of the attacks themselves. Perhaps we couldn't stop the planes from being hijacked, but we can stop the insidious hijacking of our current national experience.

It is in that spirit that the decision was made not to rewrite *Off the Cuffs*, as so many books and movies have been rewritten, to reflect the sensibilities of post-terrorist urban life, or the specific undulations of the cop/civilian dynamic during the time of the attack. That subject will find its place, I'm sure, in another book. One that is, perhaps, already being written.

NYC, 9/11/02

ACKNOWLEDGMENTS

"Psalm For Equations" © 1991 by Jack Agüeros originally appeared in *Correspondence Between the Stonehaulers* published by Hanging Loose Press in 1991. Used by permission of the author.

"The Great Flower Bust" © 2000 by Dorothy Bates originally appeared in *Creations Magazine*. Used by permission of the author.

"NYPD Blues (or the youngest homicide my father can remember)" by Ahimsa Timoteo Bodhran originally appeared in *2000: Here's to Humanity*. Used by permission of the author.

"Target Practice" © 1999 by Ahimsa Timoteo Bodhran originally appeared in *Compost*. Used by permission of the author.

"Jury Selection" © 1997 by Jeanette Clough originally appeared in *Spillway* and in *Dividing Paradise* (Laguna Beach, CA: The Inevitable Press, 1998). Used by permission of the author.

"South Central Cheap Thrill" © 2001 by Wanda Coleman originally appeared in *Mercurochrome*, Black Sparrow Press, 2001. Reprinted by permission of the author.

"Lingo" by Sarah Cortez is reprinted with permission from the publisher of *How to Undress a Cop* (Houston: Arte Publico Press—University of Houston, 2000).

"Halloween" © 1999 by Dancing Bear originally appeared in *Gravity*. Used by permission of the author.

"WTO Freewrite" © 2000 by John Paul Davis originally appeared under the title "Lines Composed A Couple Thousand Miles from Seattle" in *Columbia Poetry Review*. Used by permission of the author.

"Nightmare 9" © 1990 by Diane di Prima originally appeared in *Pieces of a Song*, City Lights, 1990. Reprinted by permission of the author.

"Great Doubters of History" copyright © 1984 by Stephen Dobyns, from *Velocities* by Stephen Dobyns. Used by permission of Penguin, a division of Penguin Putnam Inc.